ND FEMINISM

Women of Their Time: Generation, Gender Issues and Feminism

JANE PILCHER
University of Leicester

Ashgate
Aldershot • Brookfield USA • Singapore • Sydney

© Jane Pilcher 1998

All rights reserved. No part of this publication may be reproduced, stored in a retrieval system, or transmitted in any form or by any means, electronic, mechanical, photocopying, recording or otherwise without the prior permission of the publisher.

Published by
Ashgate Publishing Ltd
Gower House
Croft Road
Aldershot
Hants GU11 3HR
England

Ashgate Publishing Company
Old Post Road
Brookfield
Vermont 05036
USA

British Library Cataloguing in Publication Data
Pilcher, Jane
 Women of their time: generation, gender issues and
 feminism. - (Cardiff papers in qualitative research)
 1. Women - Great Britain - Social conditions 2. Women - Great
 Britain - History - 20th Century
 I. Title
 305.4'2'0941

Library of Congress Catalog Card Number: 98-73398

ISBN 1 84014 197 2

Printed and bound by Athenaeum Press, Ltd.,
Gateshead, Tyne & Wear.

Contents

List of tables — vi

Acknowledgements — vii

1. Gender, generation and world views — 1
2. Househusbands and breadwinning wives: Accounts of role reversal — 15
3. A man's world? Accounts of equality and discrimination — 33
4. A woman's right? Accounts of abortion — 53
5. 'Freaks' and 'normal people': Accounts of homosexuality — 73
6. 'Just a bit of fun for the men'?: Accounts of Page Three — 90
7. 'Making things better for women' or 'going over the top'?: Accounts of feminism — 108
8. Conclusions — 129

Bibliography — 139

List of tables

Table 1	Accounts of Role Reversal	20
Table 2	Accounts of the Attainment of Equality	36
Table 3	Accounts of Abortion	57
Table 4	Accounts of Homosexuality	77
Table 5	Accounts of Page Three	94
Table 6	Accounts of Feminism	112

Acknowledgements

This book is dedicated to the fifty seven women who took part in the study. The empirical research for this book was completed when I was a postgraduate student at the School of Social and Administrative Studies, University of Wales, Cardiff, funded by a University of Wales Postgraduate Studentship. I am also happy to acknowledge the support and encouragement given to me at Cardiff, particularly by Sara Delamont, Teresa Rees and Paul Atkinson. Other people introduced me to families of three generations of women and I am very grateful to them for doing so. Skilled and efficient word processing of the manuscript was provided by Jackie Swift (at Cardiff), Pat Mumby and Barbara Freer (University of Leicester). Lydia Morris and Russell Dobash examined the original PhD thesis on which this book is based and provided helpful suggestions I have tried to incorporate here. Any remaining inadequacies are fully my own responsibility.

From the beginning of the research to its completion via the writing of this book, Eddie May has been a constant when many other aspects of my life have changed. As always, he has my love and respect, as well as my thanks for helping me through the hard times. Finally, our son Jack has proved a delightful distraction, and has helped me see what the priorities in life really are.

Material used in Chapter One was first published in the *British Journal of Sociology*, vol 45, by Routledge Ltd on behalf of the London School of Economics. Copyright. The London School of Economics and Political Science, 1994. Other material contained within this chapter was first published in Chapter Eight of *Age and Generation in Modern Britain* (1995) and is reproduced here by permission of Oxford University Press. Chapters One, Two and Eight contain material first published in *Sociological Research Online*, vol 3, no 1 and is reproduced here by permission (<http://www.socresonline.org.uk/socresonline>).

September 1998

1. Gender, generation and world views

In Britain during the first three decades of the twentieth century, women struggled to obtain the vote and in 1928, finally won this key right of citizenship on the same terms as men. In Britain during the last three decades of the twentieth century, a woman became the leader of a major political party and later, Prime Minister. In the 1997 General Election, 120 women were elected as Members of Parliament, considerably more than ever before. Between the beginning of the century and its end, fundamental change has clearly occurred in women's participation in formal politics. Further, the shift from lacking the vote to holding office as Prime Minister is indicative of profound change in women's position and status elsewhere in society, including in opportunities for education and employment. There are few who would deny the key role feminism has played in bringing about this transformation.

The pace and widespread nature of change in women's status during the twentieth century means that, throughout their lives, older and younger women have experienced significantly different opportunities and constraints. As Walby explains, women of different birth cohorts have faced contrasting 'gendered opportunity structures', with dissimilar sets of options and resources, disadvantages and vulnerabilities. Consequently, women of different birth cohorts are likely to have 'different values and moralities, different political agendas and priorities' (1997: 11), not least with regard to gender issues and to feminism itself. British social scientific data on women's responses to feminism is lacking but a range of evidence on gender role attitudes in Britain and elsewhere does show that younger women are more liberal and egalitarian than older women (for example, Bell and Schwede 1985; Harding 1988; Misra and Panigrahi 1995; Roper and Labeff 1977; Scott *et al* 1996; Slevin and Ray Wingrove 1983; Thornton *et al* 1983; Witherspoon 1985).

Studies on cohort variation in attitudes to gender roles have generally been conducted via surveys, and hence with a quantitative research design. The survey approach has a number of distinct advantages as a method of examining the significance of cohort. It allows claims of representativeness and generalisability of findings, and often includes the examination of the correlation between cohort-age and other variables, including marital and employment status. The survey approach also facilitates cross-national comparisons (for example, Scott *et al* 1996) and thereby the development of explanations of changes in gender attitudes and behaviour over time and between cultures. Whilst surveys make these important contributions through providing, say, data on the proportions of each cohort 'agreeing' or 'disagreeing' with a particular questionnaire item, they are not designed to explore the equally interesting question of differences in the ways agreement or disagreement may be expressed according to cohort. Surveys give data on the 'final product' (the 'attitude') but can tell us little about how that product was formulated. Arguably, pre-coded responses 'do violence' to the richness and variety of what might otherwise be said on a particular issue. In contrast, qualitative studies, through allowing interviewees to answer in their own words, do allow a detailed examination of the vocabulary used to report responses to gender issues and an exploration of the ways in which this may vary by cohort. However, cohort studies of women's gender role attitudes using a qualitative research design remain rare. Consequently, although we know from surveys that patterns of agreement and disagreement on the issue of, say, traditional gender roles show marked differences by cohort, we have little sense of the 'reasoning', particularly in relation to gender, that results in the reported disagreement or agreement.

This book aims to fill in some of these gaps in knowledge, through examining accounts of gender issues and of feminism given by three cohorts of women in response to open-ended interview questions. In the chapters that follow, comparisons are made between the women's accounts of a range of issues which the feminist movement has advanced, including housework and the domestic division of labour, paid work and participation in public life, sexuality and reproduction, and the cultural representation of women's bodies. The comparison between the cohorts of women is extended to include an examination of their contrasting understandings of and orientations toward the organised women's movement. A key concern of this book is to show that findings from qualitative studies are an important supplement to surveys of cohort differences in women's gender role attitudes. Whilst surveys can claim representativeness and other advantages, my argument is that qualitative studies are better placed to reveal the varied and complex ways in which women of different cohorts construct gender issues and the influence cohort has on the very language they use to do so. Following on from this, and in the light of findings presented in this book, a further concern is to emphasise the importance of age as a source of diversity and difference amongst women, alongside the more widely recognised social divisions of class and ethnicity. In addition to extending sociological understanding of the ways age, via cohort, divides women and fragments their gendered experiences, the book also argues that women's accounts of gender issues and the organised women's movement are of interest and importance in their own right. Whilst there is a range of literature documenting the reflections of feminist activists on the recent history and nature of feminism (for example, Neustatter 1990; Rowland 1984; Wandor 1990), there is little evidence on the interpretations and understandings other women have of one of the most important forces of social and political change of the twentieth century. Feminism aims to change how women are perceived, but we know surprisingly little about the ways women themselves perceive feminism. Evidence on women's understandings and conceptions of gender issues and of feminism, such as presented in this book, therefore represents a valuable contribution to the debate over the status and achievements of feminism in the late twentieth century.

The study described in this book straddles several areas of sociological concern, including the saliency of gender in everyday life, the diversity of gendered identities, the nature and process of social change, the social determination of knowledge, values and beliefs, and the social significance of age. It is the latter two areas, the sociology of knowledge and the sociology of age, however, which especially shaped the conduct of the study. The remainder of this introductory chapter details the theoretical and methodological strategies followed in the study. Karl Mannheim's (1952; 1960) account of the way knowledge is determined by location in socio-historical time is discussed, including in terms of the conceptual and methodological difficulties which arise when this theory is employed in empirical settings. Of particular concern here are the entangling of age, period and cohort effects, the determination of what counts as knowledge in empirical terms, and how knowledge can be connected with socio-historical factors. Other issues considered are representativeness of the sample, generalisability of findings, and age and gender dynamics in the research setting.

Age and world views

In everyday language, the notion of a generation is commonly used as an explanation of differences in experiences and outlooks between older and younger people in society. The idea of a 'generation gap', for example, assumes clear distinctions between age groups who have grown to adulthood at different periods of historical time. In a similar way, generation is often used as a measure or marker of social change, so that a person might say 'Oh that would never have been the case a few generations ago', or 'My grandchildren's generation will expect something different from life'. Both of these everyday, popular uses of generation rest upon an assumption that the experiences and outlooks of age groups are likely to be dissimilar and, further, that such dissimilarities are understandable by reference to the different 'locations' of age groups in time. In sociology, similar links are made between a person's location in an historical social structure and their views or conceptions of the social world, via the concept of cohort. Sociologically, cohort contextualises the lives of individuals; first, within the specific interval of historical time into which they are born, grow up and old; and, second, within the company of their coevals (other individuals of the same, or similar, calendar age). As a consequence of their cohort's location in historical time, individuals and their coevals share an exposure to certain experiences and opportunities and are excluded from others.

As noted earlier, survey evidence shows the importance of age in predicting attitudes and behaviour, but such data 'only describe our problem' (Abrams 1972: 109). Theories seeking to explain why younger age groups demonstrate a tendency to hold more progressive attitudes than older age groups can be traced back to the ancient Greek philosophers (Nash 1978). More recent examples include the writings of Ortega y Gasset (Spitzer 1973) and the work of the French *Annales* school (Esler 1984). However it is Karl Mannheim's (1952) essay 'The Problem of Generations' which is widely regarded as the most systematic and fully developed treatment of the cohort aspect of the ageing process from a sociological perspective (Bengtson, Furlong and Laufer 1974). Accordingly, it is Mannheim's theory which centrally influenced the conduct of the study reported in this book. In his essay, Mannheim uses 'generation' in the sense of 'cohort'. In the following discussion, I place 'social' before all instances of Mannheim's use of 'generation'. In this manner, account is taken of the need to be careful in use of terminology, whilst links are maintained with sociological, and cultural, traditions which refer to 'generation', meaning cohort. A second reason for introducing the concept of social generation is that Mannheim's theory represents an elaboration of the concept of cohort. Recognition that individuals belong to a cohort sensitises us to the fact that their location in historical time exposes them to certain experiences, crises and events and excludes them from others. Mannheim takes this idea further. He suggests that there is a key period of exposure, namely, during youth, which has lasting ideological effects. In other words, Mannheim's argument is that, as a result of differential exposure and exclusion due to location in historical time, there exist different social generations, each having distinctive world views. This, in turn, leads people of different ages to experience the same social and cultural events differently.

Mannheim's theory of 'generations'

Mannheim's (1952) essay on cohort processes is regarded as seminal because it firmly locates cohort within socio-historical contexts, and moreover, is part of a wider sociological theory of knowledge. For Mannheim, 'knowledge' (defined by him as a style of thought or world view) is seen as socially conditioned by its location in a socio-historical structure. While discussions in the sociology of knowledge have focused on class location (Abercrombie 1980), Mannheim also identifies cohort location as a key element in the social determination of knowledge. Cohort location, like class location, points to 'certain definite modes of behaviour, feeling and thought' (Mannheim 1952: 291). In the case of class location, an individual or group's position emerges from the existence of an economic and power structure within society. The structure from which cohort location emerges is the 'existence of biological rhythm in human existence - the factors of life and death, a limited span of life, and ageing' (Mannheim 1952: 290). Although recognising the influence of biological factors, Mannheim stresses the overriding and ultimate importance of social factors, so that biology is seen to be embedded within social and historical processes. Mannheim is not, of course, implying that mere chronological contemporaneity produces a common consciousness: indeed his contention is that 'all people living at the same time do not necessarily share the same history' (Troll 1970: 201). Consequently, contemporaries may experience the same social and cultural phenomena or historical events differently.

For Mannheim, chronologically contemporaneous individuals (that is, all persons now alive) are stratified by the tendency for the formative experiences and early impressions of youth to 'coalesce into a natural view of the world' (Mannheim 1952: 298). The individual carries this with them throughout the life span. People are thus crucially influenced by the socio-historical context that predominated in their youth, and in this way, social generations have distinctive historically determined world views. Mannheim is proposing that in order to share social generational location in a sociologically meaningful sense, individuals must be born within the same historical and cultural context and be exposed to particular experiences and events that occur during their formative adult years. This is the general level of social generational location identified by Mannheim. He also provides a more specific and sophisticated analysis of social generational location. First, he recognises that geographical and cultural location will act to internally differentiate social generations, so that not every member will be exposed to exactly the same experiences. Second, he distinguishes between those social generational groupings who actually participate in the key social and cultural events of their time and place and those who do not. Thirdly, he recognises that within 'actual' social generations, there may arise differing and opposing responses to social and cultural events, in that there may develop opposing social generational 'units'.

Mannheim's discussion of social generations is integrally concerned with the issue of social change (Laufer and Bengtson 1974). Thus he maintains that the likelihood of a cohort developing a distinctive consciousness (of becoming a social generation) is dependent on the tempo of social change. In turn, social generations are regarded as a key element in the production of social change. The 'fresh contact' of new cohorts with the already existing cultural and social heritage always means a 'changed relationship of distance' and a 'novel approach in assimilating, using and developing the proffered material' (1952: 293). The progression of social change is made smoother by the presence of 'intermediary' (or buffer) social generations. The implication here is that social generations with the least difference in world views or styles of thought are always adjacent to one another, whilst those with the greatest difference are non-adjacent. In times of accelerated social change, however, when normality is disrupted, the 'new brooms' have even greater opportunity and access than the natural, gradual change over, brought about by the ageing and eventual death of all members of a cohort, allows.

The strength of cohort and social generational perspectives, such as Mannheim's, is their grasping of the defining concern of sociology as a discipline, that is, the relationship between history and biography within society (Mills 1970). Yet a range of conceptual and methodological difficulties arise when conducting empirical research on cohort and social generational processes.

The empirical study of the formation, development and retention of world views over the life course is made problematical by the complex entangling of two further 'time' elements, in addition to cohort or social generational experiences : those of ageing or individual biography and of historical or period events. Consequently, researchers may emphasize any one, or a combination, of these three central influences. Stage in life course effects, as in 'rebellious youth' or 'conservative old age', may be invoked. Period effects (historical, political or economic events or crises) may be seen to influence the world views of people of *all* ages and cohorts. Finally, explanations may centre around cohort effects, which arise from the importance of adolescent and early adulthood experiences within particular historical contexts for the formation of world views, which then persist over the life span. Empirically, it is difficult, if not impossible, to separate these three central influences (Alwin *et al* 1991).

The authors of one major recent study (Alwin *et al* 1991) favour the 'generational-persistence model' as a 'useful' summary of what is known about the formation and development of socio-political orientations over the life course. The 'generational-persistence model' (or more properly, the *cohort*-persistence model) has three components. First, the notion of a period of vulnerability to influence, occurring in late adolescence and early adulthood. Second, the notion that each new cohort experiences that time of life differently, and that there are unique residues within the individual because of those experiences. Third, the notion that, after some early period of influence and change, attitudes become crystallised and increasingly stable with age (Alwin *et al* 1991: 264). Research evidence is particularly supportive of the first and third components of the model. The importance of late adolescence as a key period of socialization is widely accepted (for review, see Braungart 1984). Moreover, research has found that people of all ages tend to report historical events and changes that occurred in their youth as especially important or meaningful (Schuman and Scott 1989; Stewart and Healy 1989). Evidence also strongly supports the notion that, once formed, world views are retained over the life span (Braungart 1984). Whilst considerable evidence exists in support of the first and third components of the model, opinion as to the long term effects of social generational or cohort experiences (the second component) is rather mixed. In reviews of available evidence, some conclude that there is a degree of support for long term social generational effects (for example, Roberts and Lang 1985), albeit 'meagre' (Alwin *et al* 1991). Others argue that little systematic evidence exists for the lasting effects of social generational experiences (for example, Schuman and Reiger 1992). Still others find that social generational differences may vary as a function of particular issues (for example, Glass *et al* 1986; Kalish and Johnson 1972; Sears 1983). Alwin *et al* (1991) reach the conclusion that evidence (including their own) supports the 'generational-persistence model'. However, they argue that the model may give too much emphasis to cohort processes and neglect other variables. They also suggest that the model may give too much emphasis to the stability of orientations over an individual's life course, in the face of evidence which shows that changes do occur over time.

The study

Despite the weakness noted above, Mannheim's work represents the strongest sociological account of cohort processes and it centrally influenced the conduct of the study reported in this book. However, putting Mannheim's theory into practice was by no means a straightforward exercise. Mannheim's (1952) essay is essentially a theoretical discussion and does not contain a model or any guidelines as to how the empirical investigation of social generational phenomena is to proceed. Yet, once Mannheim's sociology of generations is located within his wider sociology of knowledge, particular methodological approaches to the investigation of social generational phenomena are suggested.

For Mannheim, since the crucial aspect of the social conditioning of styles of thought is location in a socio-historical structure, the content and form of knowledge, of ideas, must be analysed in relation 'to the concrete setting of an historical-social situation' (Mannheim 1960: 3). Mannheim did not clearly specify exactly what constitutes knowledge in empirical terms (Dant 1991), other than suggesting that *words* (as the repositories of the *meanings* that constitute a style of thought or world view) are significant objects for study (see Mannheim 1960: 245). Similarly, within his sociology of generations, Mannheim does not provide any guidelines as to which phenomena count as 'generational consciousness'. Such shortcomings in the sociology of knowledge are addressed by Mills (1967b). Mills is critical of most sociological theories of knowledge, including Mannheim's, for their inadequate formulations of the *terms* with which they connect mind with other social factors. That is, Mills maintains that sociologies of knowledge inadequately conceptualise socio-psychological connections (1967b: 424). Mills proposes two hypotheses to remedy the situation. The first is based on Mead's social statement of the mind, and particularly his concept of the 'generalised other'. This, Mills argues, can be employed to show how societal processes enter as determinants into reflection, into the mind (1967b: 426). Mills' second hypothesis is constructed from a conjunction of the social dimensions of language with the fundamental role of language in thought (1967b: 432). The linking of the two hypotheses leads Mills to propose that, 'We may "locate" a thinker among political and social co-ordinates by ascertaining what words his [*sic*] functioning vocabulary contains and what nuances of meaning and value they embody' (Mills 1967b: 434). In this way then, Mills claims to have presented a sociological approach to reflection and knowledge that overcomes the weak socio-psychological formulations within most sociologies of knowledge (see also Dant 1991).

In another paper, Mills (1967a) elaborates on using vocabularies to 'locate' individuals. Mills argues that vocabularies can be taken to be related to the social and historical location of the utterer. Vocabularies of one group or epoch can be seen as valid at one point in time but as less acceptable at others. Mills' argument is that, in specific situations (including historically) and depending upon the 'dominant group' about whose opinion the actor cares, reports by actors are circumscribed by what is available, acceptable and conventional. Therefore, within a society, there may co-exist typical and routinized but also varying and competing vocabularies, according to the particular situation and dominant reference groups of those being studied (1967a: 449. See also Frazer 1988; Emmison and Western 1990). The investigation of the circumscribing circumstances of vocabularies, of the language employed according to historical and social situation, is posited by Mills to be a 'valuable portion' of the data to be interpreted (1967a: 452).

In the empirical study of social generational phenomena, a further difficulty remains, however: *how* are links to be made between social generational consciousness and historical time? Again, it is possible to turn to the more general solutions contained within the sociology of knowledge. According to Dant (1991), Mannheim maintains that the interpretation of meaning is central to the task of the sociology of knowledge, particularly in the sense of 'documentary meaning'. That is, interpretation of meaning with reference to the social context, so that interpretation and explanation of social generational consciousness, for example, is made in terms of its (formative) socio-historical context. Dant also notes that part of Mannheim's method in this respect is that of 'imputation', that is, an evaluation or assessment as to whether the style of thought or world view under investigation is in accord with what is known about its social context (Dant 1991: 30). There are, according to Mannheim, two levels of imputation. The first involves the reconstruction of styles of thought back to a central world view which they express, that is, the uncovering of a unity of outlook. The second level of imputation involves the assumption that the reconstructions built up from the first level are 'ideal types', which are then tested against what is known about the socio-historical context of the persons or groups being studied (Mannheim 1960: 276-277).

Once Mannheim's sociology of generations is located within his wider sociology of knowledge, a methodological approach suited to the interpretation of meaning is suggested as the most appropriate way to investigate social generational consciousness. Yet, previous research on cohorts or social generations and world views, including studies which have utilised Mannheim's theory of generations, has been of a survey nature; verbal responses have been interpreted as attitudes and the concern has been to ascertain the statistically significant degrees of difference in attitudes between cohorts. As argued above, however, Mannheim's theory of generations, in forming part of his sociology of knowledge, suggests an approach other than the survey method; specifically, one that is more suited to the interpretation of meaning. In the study reported here, therefore, the empirical investigation of social generational styles of thought or world views proceeds via taking women's sets of vocabularies[1] on gender issues and feminism as the empirical location of their knowledge. The vocabularies are assessed and interpreted in terms of time and place, that is socially and historically, using the theory of 'generations' and the method of imputation as outlined previously. The focus on vocabularies in the investigation of social generational consciousness is integral to the methodological perspective followed throughout the study.

The research method chosen to examine the influence of social generational membership on constructions of gender issues and of feminism was a qualitative, cross sectional study of three generations of adult women. That is, in-depth interviews were held with a small, multi-generational sample, at one point in time. The qualitative approach taken was a consequence of two factors. First, my understanding (via Mannheim and Mills) that an investigation of social generational consciousness should focus on words or vocabularies as the empirical location of that consciousness. Second, my attachment to the tenets of interpretive sociology: that is, a fundamental concern with the understanding of social phenomena in terms of the meaning they have for the individual and with the process of how individuals interpret and understand the social world. One means of approaching this research task is to focus on the language employed by individuals, since it is primarily in their talk that the 'understandings and definitions' (Blumer 1969) will be constituted, embodied and conveyed. As Blumer writes, the meaning social phenomena have for an individual will set 'the way in which he [*sic*] sees the object, the way in which he is prepared to act toward it, and the way in which he is ready to *talk* about it' (Blumer 1969: 11, emphasis added). As a consequence of the emphasis on the negotiation of meaning, according to context or situation, the model of social reality that interpretivist sociology holds is one that is on-going, emergent and processual. In describing women's responses to my questions in interviews as *accounts*, therefore, my intention is fully to acknowledge that reports of views held may vary according to the particular context, including the research setting itself. Comments made by some of the women during the interviews indicated that my age (twenty four at the time) and my gender were important and made a difference to what the women said to me and how they said it. For example, some women used 'we' to refer to women as a social group and would include me in that category, or they would extrapolate from their own experiences and assume that I too, as a woman, would have had similar experiences. Likewise, some younger women included me when referring to 'our generation', whilst older women described me as 'a young girl'. I have no such evidence on how the women perceived me in class or ethnic terms, or whether they perceived me to be a feminist or not.

The small scale, cross sectional design of the research reported in this book has both disadvantages and advantages. The disadvantages arise principally from the entangling of ageing effects with period and cohort effects. In cross sectional studies, the sampling of two or more age groups at one point in time means that an 'unambiguous assessment' (Buss 1974) of whether observed age differences are the effects of age, cohort or period, cannot be made. The difficulty, if not impossibility, of separating the influences of age, period and cohort is an issue in both cross sectional and longitudinal studies. Consequently, it is necessary to rely upon existing research evidence, summarised above in the generational-persistence model, as to the likely effects of these influences (see also Alwin and Scott 1996).

Studies which are concerned to explore influences on the formation and development of world views through a comparison of two or more age groups at one point in time may use samples composed either of family members or of unrelated cohorts. For this study, a multi-generational related sample was favoured. Each of the fifty seven women in the sample was a member of a family of three generations of adult women, being either mothers (born c. 1914), their daughters (born c. 1945) or their adult granddaughters (born c. 1965). Due to their differing dates of birth and the lineage gap, parent-offspring generations always belong to different birth cohorts. Such a sample acts as a strategy of contact, since one generation can provide a direct point of entry to the other generations. A related sample also means a neat and ready made cohort division, avoiding the recognised problem of where to locate cohort boundaries (Finch 1986; Rosow 1978; Spitzer 1973)[2]. Using related samples does, however, introduce the complicating factor of family socialization. Again, it is necessary to rely on the existing research literature to make assumptions about the influence of this factor. Such evidence points to the importance of family socialization and to the likelihood of finding a degree of similarity within families (Alwin et al 1991; Glass et al 1986). However, in a study of attitudes to gender roles (Slevin and Ray Wingrove 1983), major differences prevailed between generations, dominating any tendency toward intrafamily similarities.

The sampling strategy employed in the study is best described as an 'opportunistic' one. The families of women were contacted through meeting older women at Pensioners' Clubs and Day Centres for Elderly People, via personal contacts who introduced me to multi-generational families of women, and via snowballing from these two sources. The family member who was first contacted acted as a 'gatekeeper' to the other generations. Only if the participation of all three generations of women was assured were families accepted into the sample. An additional criterion was that all three had to live within a defined geographical area, since restricted time and finances precluded my travelling great distances. In qualitative research, the concern is with detail and depth of information, which strengthens the validity of the study by reflecting informants' responses, but which also raises the problems of representativeness and generalisability (Hakim 1987; see also Hammersley 1989). Clearly, given the small-size and opportunistic nature of the sample, I can not claim that my findings are representative or generalisable. Where nationally representative data on age group differences is available, however, I am able to make comparisons with my findings. Data from the *British Social Attitudes* surveys proved particularly useful here.

The sample of women whose accounts of gender issues and feminism provide the data for this study lived in urban areas in South Wales. The majority were born and had lived most of their lives in this same area. All of the women were white. The overwhelming majority of both the oldest and middle generation women reported holding no educational qualifications (although three of the middle generation had gained degrees as mature students). The majority of the youngest generation held educational qualifications gained as sixteen year old school leavers. Only four of the nineteen women of the youngest generation had studied (or were studying) in further or higher education. The social class of the women was established using the Registrar General's *Classification of Occupations* (OPCS 1980)[3]. Using this classification scheme to categorise the women's own occupations, a majority (56%) were categorised as 'middle class'. Most fell into the intermediate (Class IIIn) category (38.5%), via their work in offices and shops, with a smaller proportion (17.5%) working in managerial level jobs (Class II). A majority of the male partners (or fathers, in the case of non-cohabiting youngest generation women) of the women were categorised as working class, via their work in skilled, semi-skilled or unskilled manual occupations (56%). Most of these men (47%) fell into the skilled manual category (Class IIIm). A significant proportion (30%) of the male partners/fathers held managerial positions (Class II). Overall, if the women's own occupations are used to determine their social class, the sample becomes more middle class than working class in character. If the 'derived' principle of classification is used, whereby the women's social class is determined by that of the occupation of male partners/fathers, then the sample becomes more working class in character. This analysis shows the complexity of household and family class relationships and underlines the necessity for class analysis and theory to be reconceptualised to fully take account of gender. Ultimately, however, whichever principle of classification is used, the single largest grouping in this sample is Class III (49% under both measures) and thus the sample is bunched around the middle of the social class scale.

Each woman was individually interviewed in 1989. Interviews were tape recorded and fully transcribed, since having a full record of the women's responses was central to the research task of focusing on words and vocabularies. The interviews were informal, in that the sequence and wording of questions were flexible. The style can be described as that of a 'guided conversation' (Lofland and Lofland 1984). Analysis of the interview data centered around the intensive comparison of words and phrases and from this, sets of vocabularies were discovered to be employed in discussion of topics raised in the interviews. The topics or issues raised in the interviews, whilst not aiming to define 'gender issues', were intended to reflect concerns which have been central to the feminist agenda, both recently and historically. These include issues relating to gender in the domestic context, in paid work, in public life and politics, in sexuality and reproduction, and in culture.

In the chapters that follow, the aim is to suggest how the contrasting gendered life courses faced by the women have influenced their understandings of gender issues, via an analysis of the range of vocabularies they employed in the interview setting. Necessarily, therefore, the women's own words feature prominently throughout. The women are, more or less, allowed to 'speak for themselves', whilst a series of themes are accumulated (see also Plummer 1983). Quotations from the women are accompanied by a pseudonym and by an abbreviated reference to indicate their generation. Throughout, the oldest generation is taken as the 'index' generation (Troll 1970) and data presented invariably first begins with an examination of their accounts, followed by those of the middle and then the youngest generation. In order to provide a background with which to interpret the women's accounts, and to establish their likely formative historical contexts in relation to the particular gender issue under focus, each chapter includes an overview constructed from available historical and sociological evidence and relevant material from the women's own reported life histories.

Chapter Two explores the women's constructions of gendered roles and responsibilities in the home and in paid work, in the face of changed expectations about men's involvement in housework/childcare and women's involvement in paid work. In Chapter Three, issues of equality, inequality and discrimination outside the home are the main focus. The issue of reproductive rights is explored in Chapter Four, through examining the women's accounts of abortion. For feminism, sexuality has long been a key gender issue, and in Chapter Five, the women's constructions of 'homosexuality' (male and female) are the focus whilst Chapter Six reports on the women's responses to representations of women's bodies, in particular 'Page 3' of *The Sun* newspaper. The penultimate chapter moves away from an examination of the women's constructions of gender issues to their understandings of and responses to the organised women's movement and its activists. The concluding chapter identifies the 'unity of outlook' of each cohort, or their 'social generational consciousness', suggested by the contrasting types of vocabularies each cohort invariably employed across the range of gender issues. An assessment is made as to the implications of the study, including for understandings of the social significance of age and for knowledge of responses to gender issues and to feminism.

Notes

1. By vocabularies, I mean sets or ways of talking, which comprise distinctive words or phrases, and which embody the meanings placed by the utterer upon that which is the topic or focus of discussion.

2. The process of locating boundaries was not, however, completely arbitrary. Since the focus of concern was social generational influences on accounts of gender issues and feminism, the youngest generation in the sample had to have grown to adulthood and been exposed to the significant social and cultural changes in women's lives that have occurred since the 1960s, following the 'second wave' of the feminist movement. This set their age range at approximately seventeen to the upper twenties. The age bands of the older two generations in and of themselves were not set or fixed; basically, they came as they were.

3. Using this classification scheme to determine women's own occupational class has its disadvantages, because it is insensitive to the types of occupations women are to be found in. Classification schemes have been developed which attempt to address such problems, but they have yet to be widely adopted (see Abbott and Sapsford 1987).

2. Househusbands and breadwinning wives: Accounts of role reversal

Living together in daily life requires the completion, on a regular and ongoing basis, of a range of tasks such as food preparation, washing clothes, cleaning and, often, looking after children. In Britain, this domestic work arising from daily living has traditionally been undertaken by women rather than men, and for the most part, on an unpaid basis. The allocation of responsibility to women for domestic work is widely argued to be a key factor in the generalised inequalities women face in society compared to men, particularly in paid work (see Walby 1990 for review). Despite changes over time in the structure of households, most people live or have lived in a family and therefore have direct experience of the ways in which routine household work gets done and by whom. In addition to being central to theoretical explanations of gender inequalities, therefore, the issue of domestic work is also a concrete, non-abstract concern, close to the everyday lives of individuals, particularly women, who mostly have responsibility for it. For these reasons, the issue of domestic work suggested itself as key one in the investigation of women's accounts of gender issues, contrasted by cohort. In line with the analytical approach followed throughout the study, this chapter begins by providing a socio-historical context for the women's accounts of domestic work responsibilities, using historical and sociological evidence as well as the women's own reported experiences and descriptions of the gendered nature of domestic work in past and present times. The main part of the chapter focuses on the women's constructions of domestic work responsibilities, via an analysis of their responses to 'role reversal'.

Domestic work, gendered responsibilities and social change

In the early part of the twentieth century, evidence suggests that for most families, a gendered division of labour was the norm (see Morris 1990; Pahl 1984 for review). Men primarily had responsibility for the financial provision of households and women for the management and performance of domestic tasks necessary for the day to day running of the household (for example Roberts 1984; for evidence on Wales, see Crook 1982 and Red Flannel Films 1982). Some oral history evidence reveals that men did participate in domestic work (for example, Thompson 1975; Lummis 1982) but that this was infrequent and generally restricted to periods of temporary domestic crises. Evidence from sociological studies undertaken in the years after World War Two (for example Mogey 1956; Dennis, Henriques and Slaughter [1956] 1969; Zweig 1952) suggests that there remained a clear demarcation of the roles of men and women, with men having the role of 'breadwinner' for the household and women having responsibility for the day to day running of the household. Where married women had some financial input into the household through paid work, husbands may have slightly increased their involvement in domestic work. However, this generally took the form of 'helping' their wives to do the domestic work, which remained the woman's responsibility (Zweig 1952).

The historical and sociological evidence on the domestic division of labour in the first and middle part of the twentieth century is matched by the accounts of 'the past' given by the women in the study. A minority of women did say that men undertook housework in the past on occasion, but across the three cohorts, the central feature in the descriptions of the past was the predominance of traditional gender roles and responsibilities. For example, some women spoke of the gendered expectations surrounding the roles of women and men, so that boys were brought up not to do housework whilst girls were.

> My mother brought us girls up to do the work while my brothers went to work...They came home and waited for us, do you understand, to get the food...They expected the women in the house to do it.
>
> Doreen Owens, aged 70 (G1)

Home was where men returned in order to be fed and rested after their day at work. The provision and serving of food was a recurrent feature of descriptions (see also Murcott 1987).

> My mother used to say, 'Oh your father will be home soon. We must get so and so done...and get his meal on the table, you know...With my father, he never did a thing...It was so different then.
>
> Doris Ascote, aged 72 (G1)

...Men used to just come home and whatever, sit down and have their food put in front of them.

Miriam Powell, aged 43 (G2)

In accounts of past times, men were described as the 'breadwinners' and providers for the family, whilst the 'place' of women was firmly recognised to be in the home, being a 'good housewife and a good mother' (Rene Evans, aged 82, G1). Women were said to rarely work outside of the home. The hierarchical power relationships between men and women underpinning these gendered roles and responsibilities were also described. Women 'waited' on men, were 'domineered' by men, were always the 'inferior race'. Men were the 'bosses' and the 'masters'. As Sybil Richards (aged 71, G1) described it, 'A man was the king, always, and the woman was the slave'.

The accounts of domestic divisions of labour in 'the past' showed few qualitative differences between the cohorts, leading to a conclusion that there is a vocabulary of this past that is widely shared. It may, of course, be that the women were not talking about the 'same' past. Women of the oldest cohort may have been describing a situation that they associated with their own mothers or grandmothers. The youngest cohort may have associated the past they spoke of with their grandmothers' earlier lives. Even taking this point into account, however, merely serves to make the uniformity of the descriptions of gendered roles and responsibilities in 'the past' all the more remarkable.

In Britain, the end of the 1950s and in particular the 1960s, saw an unprecedented rise in the proportion of married women in paid employment, including in Wales, where historically women have had lower rates of participation in the formal labour market than women in other parts of Britain (Brennen, Cooney and Pollins 1954; Rosser and Harris 1965; Winckler 1987a, 1987b). Studies of family life began to suggest that the pattern of the domestic division of labour was undergoing change (Bott [1957] 1971; Young and Willmott [1973] 1975; Rosser and Harris 1965; Gavron [1966] 1983). Findings were argued to indicate that jointness and equality had become, or would shortly become, the predominant pattern. Since then, however, much evidence has been ranged against such optimistic conclusions about the extent and significance of changes in the domestic division of labour. Despite women's increased participation in the paid labour market, and the popularity of the notion of the 'New Man', it is women rather than men who remain responsible for unpaid domestic work (for example, Brannen and Moss 1991; Morris 1985a, 1985b, 1985c; Mansfield and Collard 1988; Martin and Roberts 1984; Pahl 1984; Warde and Hetherington 1993; Gershuny 1997).There is some evidence of an increase in the participation of men in domestic work but, put simply, women's increased participation in the labour market has not been matched by men's increased participation in domestic work and an imbalance remains. Moreover, this has taken place against the changed nature of domestic work, which means that despite (or indeed because of) the introduction of technological gadgets, the work has become more demanding due to rising standards (Cowan 1989).

The debate over the extent and significance of change in domestic divisions of labour was reflected in the women's own accounts of the present, in that these showed less uniformity and consensus than was evident in their accounts of the past. Although some women of the oldest cohort said that 'it doesn't always work out that way' (Nora Lestor, aged 72, G1), more said that there had been considerable change over time. Men 'today' were described as doing more housework and childcare than previously: 'They'll do anything now' (Ivy Keating, aged 87, G1). The middle cohort also described increases in men's participation in domestic work over time, but more often the change was described as partial, so that not all women had 'enlightened husbands' (Angharad Baker, aged 50, G2) and women's responsibilities for housework and childcare remained basically the same. The youngest cohort also showed a tendency to say that change had been partial. Men are 'still reluctant' to do housework, whilst women are 'still tied down with doing all the housework all the time' (Ruth Richards, aged 17, G3).

Research evidence, and many of the women's own accounts, indicate that a gendered division of labour remains common in contemporary Britain, with women retaining primary responsibility for and undertaking the bulk of the domestic work. The evidence does show that the degree of imbalance between women and men in households varies according to factors such as stage in the family life course and the employment status of the woman partner. However, in comparison with the first half of this century, when married women were not generally employed outside of the home and undertook the bulk of the work within it, the gendered division of labour can be argued to have become less, rather than more, equal over time. Explanations for the resilience of a gendered division of labour centre around 'a web of constraining influences' (Morris 1987), including gender role and family ideology, the gendering of paid work and the policies and practices of the agencies of the welfare state.

Role reversal: putting gender 'out of place'

The 'web of constraining influences' which militate against fundamental and widespread change in gendered divisions of labour means that, despite probable increases in recent years, households operating on a system of 'role reversal', with the woman as the full time paid worker and breadwinner, and the man as the unpaid domestic worker in the home, remain very much a rarity. Morris (for example, 1985a) has shown that even in the context of men's redundancy and subsequent unemployment, strong social pressures remain which hinder the renegotiation of the domestic division of labour. Role reversal households are, then, unconventional and remarkable. On a symbolic level, role reversal households represent a challenge to the various components of traditional gender role ideology, including ideas about motherhood and children's 'needs', dependent femininity, and men as providers and heads of households. For some couples, reversing roles may be a conscious choice, precisely because it puts gender 'out of place' through its radical alteration of conventional gender and generational relationships at the level of the household. For other couples, a reversal of roles may be forced upon them and reflect changes in opportunities faced by some women and men in the labour market. Whether through choice or force of circumstance, role reversal disturbs the conventional patterns of responsibilities and power relations between women and men which are central to the performance of masculinity and femininity. For this reason, role reversal presents itself as an ideal issue through which to examine accounts of the gendered domestic division of labour and how these differ qualitatively between cohorts.

In wording the interview question on role reversal, I deliberately did not use the term 'role reversal'. I anticipated that some of the women might have been unfamiliar with the term and further, that if individual women were familiar with it, the term itself might be associated with pre-conceived notions. The question was therefore phrased as follows: *'What would you think of a marriage or a relationship where the man stayed at home and did the housework and looked after the children, if there were any; and the woman was the one who went out to work full time?'*. The accounts that the three cohorts of women gave in response to this question were broadly categorised into 'hostile' and 'sympathetic'. Table One shows the distribution of accounts categorised as hostile and sympathetic by cohort. The majority (12) of the oldest cohort gave accounts hostile to role reversal, whilst the majority of the two younger cohorts (13 in each case) gave sympathetic accounts.

Table 1   **Accounts of Role Reversal**

	Oldest Cohort	Middle Cohort	Youngest Cohort	TOTAL
'Hostile'	12	5	6	23
'Sympathetic'	6	13	13	32
No data	1	1	-	2
TOTAL	19	19	19	57

Supporting evidence for the pattern of cohort differences shown in Table One is provided by the 1985 *British Social Attitudes* survey. The survey made use of a similar statement in order to tap attitudes to gender roles and the traditional pattern of the domestic division of labour: 'A husband's job is to earn the money; a wife's job is to look after the home and the family'. Patterns of 'agreement' and 'disagreement' with this statement showed marked differences by age group. Thus, whilst 21% of women aged 55 and over 'agreed strongly' with the statement, 14% of women aged 35-54 and 8% of women aged 18-24 did so. In contrast, 24% of women aged 18-24 'disagreed strongly' with the statement, compared to 25% of the 35-54 year olds and 12% of those aged 55 and over (Witherspoon 1985: 93, table 3.13).

The data presented in Table One show important cohort differences on role reversal, but 'head counting' cannot, of course, reveal the richness and variety of what the women said on the issue. It is to the analysis of the contrasting vocabularies used by the cohorts of women that I now turn. Four types of vocabularies were present in the women's accounts of role reversal and the core issue of the gendered responsibility for domestic work that it tapped in to. These vocabularies were labelled as *traditional, individualism, equality* and *structural constraints*.

'Hostile' accounts of role reversal

Twenty three accounts were categorised as comprised of 'hostile' vocabularies, with women of the oldest cohort giving twice as many hostile accounts (12) as either of the younger two cohorts. Whether given by the oldest, middle or youngest cohort, 'hostile' accounts were constructed using a vocabulary of traditional gender roles (henceforth, a *traditional vocabulary*). There were differences, however, between the cohorts in the content of this vocabulary.

In the hostile accounts given by the oldest cohort, role reversal was something they said they did not like or, in two accounts, had difficulty even imagining. In reflecting upon role reversal, the women of this cohort identified the unusual circumstances which would bring men in to the domestic environment, such as their unemployment or ill health. For example,

> ...Unless it was that the husband *couldn't* find a job and the wife was able to work.
>
> Nancy Caswell, aged 69 (G1)

> ...If it was a case of the husband not being able to go out to work, if there was something wrong with him, well, all right. That's fair enough...Somebody's got to be the breadwinner.
>
> Irene Harvey, aged 62 (G1)

Six women made reference to such forces of circumstance, under which role reversal might be countenanced. Even so, in some of the women's accounts, a man's incapacity to be a breadwinner did not automatically mean that he should then become completely responsible for domestic work. For Nancy Caswell, Agnes Baker and Dora Griffiths, men could 'help' their wives if they themselves were not working but, 'not completely look after the family and the house' (Agnes Baker, aged 78, G1). Moreover, two women of this cohort expressed a concern over the effect of role reversal on the man's feelings and status. For example,

> I don't think I would like to go out [to work] and leave my husband at home doing work.// Well, it makes the husband think he's not looking after you properly, really.
>
> Irene Harvey, aged 62 (G1)

The conditions under which role reversal might be acceptable (a man's unemployment or inability to work, his 'helping' rather than having complete responsibility for domestic work and, in both cases, 'if the man was prepared to do it' (Doris Ascote, aged 72, G1), are core characteristics of a vocabulary of hostility which presented role reversal as an infringement of traditional gender roles. This is clearest in the account's of five women which contained the phrases 'a man's place' and/or 'a woman's place'. For example,

> Actually, I don't agree with that. I got to be truthful...a man's place is in work, provide and a woman's work is to have her babies and look after them and look after the home.
>
> Sybil Richards, aged 71 (G1)

> No, I wouldn't like that. I think a man's place is in work. No, I don't think I'd like that at all.
>
> Dora Griffiths, aged 68 (G1)

> Well, I'm not at all in favour...I think a woman's place is in the home.
>
> Rose Jessop, aged 73 (G1)

Apart from Sybil Richards and Dora Griffiths, the women specified the 'place' of the woman, particularly as a mother to children, rather than the 'place' of the man. Five other accounts given in response to role reversal, did not contain the references to women's and men's 'place', but nevertheless made explicit reference to traditional gender roles. Here, the role of men as breadwinners featured more strongly:

> I don't think it's right.//...I think you get married and your husband will keep you or work for you.
>
> Ivy Keating, aged 87 (G1)

> Well, I just wouldn't like it.//...when the husband brings the money home, that's great, ain't it.
>
> Irene Harvey, aged 62 (G1)

> We have been brought up with the man being the breadwinner, primarily. That was the norm when I was young.
>
> Nancy Caswell, aged 69 (G1)

Ivy Keating, quoted above, was the only woman of the oldest cohort who gave an indication that her vocabulary of the 'proper' roles of men and women was perhaps unconventional or unacceptable in contemporary society. After saying about husbands 'keeping' their wives, she added that this was probably 'an old fashioned idea, I suppose'.

Overall, then, in the twelve hostile accounts given by the oldest cohort, role reversal was portrayed as an infringement of a woman's place as homemaker and mother and, especially, of a man's place as breadwinner. The role and status of men was a central feature in these women's accounts of role reversal, evident in their initial reflections upon the forces of circumstance which might bring men in to the domestic environment and in their expressions of concern about how a man would feel when faced with a domestic role. Throughout their accounts of role reversal, a traditional vocabulary was to the fore, including several occurrences of the phrases 'a man's place' and 'a woman's place'.

A minority of accounts (five) given about role reversal by the middle cohort were hostile in content, and all drew upon a traditional vocabulary. For example:

> I wouldn't like it. I wasn't brought up that way...the man went out to work and the woman stayed at home with the children.
> Susan Griffiths, aged 44 (G2)

> Wouldn't like it.//...it's a man's place to go out to work.
> Valerie Harvey, aged 40 (G2)

Two women were only prepared to countenance the idea of role reversal under circumstances which forced the man to be in a domestic environment, that is, if he was unemployed or unable to work due to ill health. Two others explained their antipathy to role reversal on the grounds that men are incompetent at housework, a feature not present in the oldest cohort's accounts: 'Some men, they still don't do it the way you do it, you know' (Miriam Powell, aged 43, G2). Valerie Harvey (aged 40, G2) also doubted whether her husband would do the housework to the same standard as she did, if he had responsibility for it. When I then suggested to her that he might soon learn, she replied that he *should* not. She was suggesting that it would not be proper for him to gain a high level of competency in housework, because this would violate traditional gender roles. As in the hostile accounts of the oldest cohort, these women's hostile accounts were constructed around a focus on *men's* roles and status.

The six hostile accounts of the youngest cohort were also comprised of a traditional vocabulary. None of these women had children themselves and only one was cohabiting or married. A particular feature, present in four accounts, was the referencing of women's roles as mothers. For example:

> No. I wouldn't like that. I'd like to be there with the children.
> Rhian Keating, aged 24 (G3)

> ...(I think) the mother should look after the child...the child needs the mother more really.
> Sharon Owens, aged 18 (G3)

As suggested by Scott *et al* (1996), for younger women, opposition to role reversal may be more acceptable or permissable if expressed in terms of children's needs, rather than men's needs, as in the older cohort's accounts. However, the role and status of men did feature in the hostile accounts given by the youngest cohort. One woman objected to role reversal on the grounds of men's incompetency in domestic work. She cited media representations of role reversal as her evidence:

> I don't know about that [role reversal]. I think the woman should stay at home and look after the children and do the housework...I don't think the men should stay at home because I don't think they could cope. Like, I saw this film on T.V., 'Mr. Mum', and the man stayed at home and looked after the children and that, and it didn't work out.
>
> Mandy Mitchell, aged 17 (G3)

In two other hostile accounts, reference was made to the feelings and status of men who had a domestic role, given that this would be an infringement of their traditional roles as men:

> I think it would be humiliating for a man...Like, if I was a man, I wouldn't like to be kept.
>
> Elaine Griffiths, aged 19 (G3)

> I don't think the man would like it all that much, would he. Men like to go out to do the work, rather than stay home and do the housework.
>
> Lorraine Morgan, aged 19 (G3)

The vocabulary thus presents role reversal as a threat to masculine identity, whilst women who stay at home do not have to 'swallow their pride' or feel humiliated at 'being kept'.

There were two features present in the hostile accounts of the youngest cohort which were not found in other hostile accounts. Wendy Caswell acknowledged that her antipathy to role reversal was not in line with a feminist stress on equality:

> For me personally, I wouldn't like it...you know, women's lib. and all that kind of stuff but I would want to be with the children.
>
> Wendy Caswell, aged 22 (G3)

The second feature unique to the youngest cohort's hostile accounts of role reversal was an awareness, in two cases, of the gendered structure of the labour market which militates against role reversal. Lorraine Morgan (aged 19, G3) said that she would not be able to 'earn enough money' in her line of work (office worker) to enable her to reverse roles. Similarly, Wendy Caswell (aged 22, G3) said that 'It will always be that men have got better jobs', so 'not a lot' stay home and look after the children. Here, rather than expressing their hostility to role reversal in ideological terms, the women are identifying structural constraints which inhibit role reversal, and make it an impractical option for many households.

'Sympathetic' accounts of role reversal

A majority (32) of accounts were categorised as comprised of sympathetic vocabularies, with women of the oldest cohort giving half as many sympathetic accounts as either of the younger two cohorts. As the following analysis shows, sympathetic accounts were constructed with several vocabularies, with noticeable differences between the cohorts.

Six women of the oldest cohort gave sympathetic accounts of role reversal, and specified the sorts of circumstances which might lead to this unusual arrangement. Two women, although favourable to the idea of role reversal, used a traditional vocabulary, with the man as the main focus of their concern.

> If there was no work about for the man, yes...As long as the man wasn't demoted, do you understand me, because of that, you know.
>
> Doreen Owens, aged 70 (G1)

> Well, to me, I think that's a good idea. If he wants to do that.
>
> Elsie Farrall, aged 74 (G1)

In these two accounts, the forces of circumstance which would bring a man in to a domestic environment are identified and concern is expressed as to the consequences for his masculine status, if he was prepared to do it. In contrast, the other four sympathetic accounts given by women of this cohort had the position and status of the woman as a primary focus. In two accounts, circumstances where the woman partner had a 'good job', earning more money than the man, were specified. For example:

> I don't see as it makes any difference really, if the wife has a good job...
>
> Yvonne Daniels, aged 75 (G1)

Three women conveyed their views on role reversal via telling 'success stories' of couples known to them who had reversed roles, either because the woman partner had 'a better job', 'earned more' or had 'a very important job' compared to the man. Direct knowledge of successes therefore seemed an important factor influencing the sympathetic construction of role reversal by the oldest cohort of women. In stressing the practicality of the arrangement according to the circumstances faced by the couple involved, the women drew upon a vocabulary of individualism.

The middle cohort of women were twice as supportive in their accounts of role reversal than were the oldest cohort. They too specified the circumstances under which role reversal might occur, thereby suggesting that it is an unusual way of dividing responsibilities between women and men. However, in contrast to hostile accounts, the identification of circumstances was accompanied by clear approval of role reversal. In five of the thirteen supportive accounts, approval of the idea of role reversal was accompanied by reference to the relative earning power of the couple. For example:

> Well, if the woman has got a better job and is bringing more money into the house. And if they are agreeable, I don't see anything wrong.
>
> Angela Farrall, aged 44 (G2)

> That's fine, it's sensible. I think the one who has the greatest earning power ought to do the work.
>
> Rosemary Thomas, aged 46 (G2)

> Well, I certainly don't see anything wrong with it. I mean, if the woman could earn more money than the man. Well then, that is fair enough.
>
> Carol Mitchell, aged 38 (G2)

In these examples, the practicality of the arrangement is stressed according to the paid work circumstances a couple might face. This vocabulary of individualism, where the main feature is the suitability of the arrangement, according to the circumstances, preferences and/or character, of the particular couple concerned, was a prominent one in the sympathetic accounts of this cohort. For example:

> Fine, if it suits them and they are happy...
> Judith Ascote, aged 48 (G2)

> That's fine, if they are happy doing that.
> Janice Caswell, aged 44 (G2)

> I wouldn't mind. I think my husband's got more patience than I have...I think he would be quite willing to stay at home.
> Rita Parry, aged 42 (G2)

Unlike the oldest cohort, no women of this cohort gave a sympathetic account of role reversal via a traditional vocabulary. In other words, none expressed concerns about the feelings and status of men in a situation of role reversal (although Angela Farrall (aged 44, G2) did say that she was unsure how men in general would feel about having a domestic role), nor were the circumstances of the man's unemployment or inability to work specified. Of the middle cohort, Janet Morgan (aged 47, G2) was alone in expressing her positive assessment of the idea of role reversal in terms of the principle of equality, saying '...Yes, it's equality, isn't it really. Yes, I have got no objections to that'. With these exceptions, women of this cohort constructed their sympathetic accounts of role reversal with a vocabulary of individualism.

The thirteen sympathetic accounts of role reversal given by the youngest cohort also specified the sorts of circumstances which would lead to role reversal. In six accounts, sympathy for role reversal was expressed through referencing the relative earning power and employability of the couple. For example:

> That's fair, I mean, if she can earn more. If he can't get a job and she finds one, I don't see the difference.
> Rebecca Daniels, aged 29 (G3)

> I think it's all right...if the wife have [sic] got a good job and the man hasn't got a job, then there is no point in them both being home.
> Denise Nicholl, aged 27 (G3)

> Fine. It depends, you know, normally the man can earn a better wage. But if the woman can earn a good wage, why not?
> Bethan Parry, aged 24 (G3)

In these accounts, it was especially the status of the woman partner's job that was cited as important (six examples), with the enforced circumstances of men's unemployment cited only twice. In Bethan Parry's account (above) the structural constraints which militate against role reversal are identified (*a vocabulary of structural constraints*). Rather than reflecting on the circumstances that might bring men in to the domestic environment (a feature of the oldest cohort's accounts), for these women of the youngest cohort, the focus was the circumstances which encourage women to continue in paid work. Concern for damaged masculinity was expressed by one woman, who said that a man in a role reversal situation would have to 'swallow his pride' but that if he did reverse roles, this would be 'to his credit' (Lindsay Farrall, aged 20, G3). Otherwise, the status and feelings of men did not feature. Instead, there was a concern with the happiness and needs of the couple:

> Oh, I think that was great...if you've got that kind of relationship.
>
> Karen Lestor, aged 29 (G3)
>
> Well, if they are happy, that's fine. If it suited them, that's fine.
>
> Isabel Ascote, aged 21 (G3)

In speaking of the practicalities of role reversal, according to the circumstances, character and preferences of the couple involved, these women employed a vocabulary of individualism.

A distinctive feature of this cohort's accounts was an explicit interpretation of role reversal as a challenge to traditional gender roles or as an example of gender equality in practice. For example,

> Good.//...Well, long enough that women have stayed in the home.
>
> Ruth Richards, aged 17 (G3)
>
> I agree that women should have equality.
>
> Kirsty Harvey, aged 19 (G3)

One other woman of this cohort employed a similar vocabulary in her account of role reversal. Hayley Baker (aged 23, G3) explained her view that role reversal was a good idea 'on the surface' because it is something that men do not usually do and that it would therefore be good for society as a whole. These are examples of a vocabulary of equality, where role reversal is presented as a 'good thing' on ideological grounds.

Conclusions

This chapter has examined accounts of the gendered division of labour, given in response to an interview question on the issue of role reversal. The data show that the women in the study responded in contrasting ways to role reversal. Women in the oldest cohort tended to give hostile accounts, mostly portraying role reversal as a violation of traditional gender roles. Women in the younger cohorts tended to give sympathetic accounts, where role reversal was mostly presented as an acceptable arrangement, according to the particular circumstances faced by a couple. The qualitative analysis of the accounts of role reversal focused on the contrasting types of vocabulary used. Four types of vocabularies were present in the women's accounts of role reversal and the core issue of the gendered responsibility for domestic work that it tapped in to. These vocabularies were labelled as *traditional, individualism, equality* and *structural constraints*. Of these, the traditional and the individualism types were the most frequently employed.

A *traditional vocabulary* was predominantly used in hostile accounts, and was especially made use of by women of the oldest cohort. It presented role reversal as a violation of traditional gender roles, responsibilities and power relationships. It contained descriptions of traditional and conventional gender roles and responsibilities, and included the prescriptive use of the phrases 'a man's place' and 'a woman's place'. References were made to forces of circumstance which might place men in a domestic context, such as their unemployment or ill health, and concern was expressed over the detrimental effects on masculinity. Doubts as to men's competency in domestic work also formed part of this vocabulary. In essence, then, a traditional vocabulary portrayed role reversal as an infringement of traditional, conventional and 'proper' gendered roles and responsibilities, particularly from a man's point of view. Gender was presented as a legitimate basis on which to determine roles and responsibilities, and in a prescriptive and inflexible manner.

A *vocabulary of individualism* was predominantly used in accounts sympathetic to role reversal, and especially by the middle and youngest cohorts. Its main feature was the emphasis on the practicality of role reversal according to the paid work circumstances, preferences and characters of the couple concerned. Within this vocabulary, role reversal was presented as a choice that should be made on practical grounds, according to the employment status and prospects of each partner in a couple, including their earnings potential. The gender of each partner seemed irrelevant; rather, role reversal was a matter of what 'suited' the particular couple and their particular circumstances.

The *equality vocabulary* presented role reversal as an example of gender equality or feminist principles in practice. It was only used by women in the younger cohorts and mostly in their sympathetic accounts of role reversal. Here, role reversal was supported on ideological grounds, and portrayed as representing a valid challenge to traditional and conventional divisions of labour, which disadvantage women. Within this vocabulary, therefore, gender was suggested as a significant, if illegitimate, basis on which experiences and opportunities are shaped. Where an equality vocabulary was used by women in their hostile accounts, the status of role reversal as a challenge to gender inequality was recognised but not felt to be appropriate to their own preferences or circumstances.

A *vocabulary of structural constraints* was only found in hostile and sympathetic accounts given by the youngest cohort. This vocabulary identified the structural pressures which make role reversal very difficult to achieve. In particular, the gendered nature of paid work was said to make it unlikely that a woman would have the sort of job to enable her to be a 'breadwinner', rather than her partner. This type of vocabulary suggests a recognition of wider structures of gender inequality which constrain choices and options available to couples at the level of the household. Gender is invoked as an important determinant of opportunity and as highly relevant to the household strategy a couple might develop.

Two types of vocabulary, traditional and individualism, were made use of by all three cohorts. However, the traditional vocabulary was employed mostly by the oldest cohort and the vocabulary of individualism mostly by the middle and youngest cohorts. Vocabularies of equality and, especially, structural constraints were not used at all by the oldest cohort, but especially by the youngest cohort. Within sociology, vocabularies are argued to reflect the context of their use, including the wider context of socio-historical location, via life course and cohort membership. For the oldest cohort, therefore, using a vocabulary which constructed role reversal as a violation of traditional gender roles, responsibilities and relationships reflected their socialisation experiences and life courses lived within a particular gendered socio-historical structure. The historical context of these women's life courses was one where men only undertook limited household work, married women had a limited involvement in paid work and where a marked gendered division of labour was the norm. According to the women themselves, their own earlier involvement in paid work was intermittent, broken (if not ended) by marriage or children. They also reported on their long held responsibility for domestic work, which often continued after their husbands' retirement (see also Mason 1987). Data on these women's accounts of men's involvement in housework, published elsewhere, showed that they were concerned to specify the circumstances and extent of men's participation. Their talk showed them to be resistant to the substantial involvement of men in the domestic sphere and to hold low expectations about men's domestic work activities (Pilcher 1994). In the context of these women's socio-historical experiences, therefore, talking about 'a man's place' and 'a woman's place', noting the force of circumstances that would bring a man in to the domestic context and expressing concern about the effects this would have on his masculinity, were all appropriate, valid and acceptable ways of talking about role reversal. For the same reasons, talking about role reversal in terms of individualism was not an acceptable or, in the case of equality or structural constraints, possibly even available, vocabulary, for most women of this cohort. An important contingency affecting the sympathetic construction of role reversal for the oldest cohort was direct knowledge of role reversal 'success': three out of six women giving sympathetic accounts of role reversal told 'success stories', employing a vocabulary of individualism in the process.

In the accounts of the two younger cohorts, a traditional vocabulary was less evident, both in terms of prominence and explicitness. Conversely, an individualistic vocabulary (citing practicality of circumstances, personal needs and happiness) was more frequently employed. These cohort differences in use of vocabulary also allow an interpretation along the lines of discursive acceptability and availability arising from cohort location in historical gendered opportunity structures. The two younger cohorts experienced a different socio-historical context to that faced by the oldest cohort, including in terms of changed expectations about married women and paid work, with knock-on effects for expectations about men and domestic work. Married women have increasingly participated in the formal labour market in greater numbers since the 1950s and, as Martin and Roberts (1984) have argued, we should therefore expect to find differences between older and younger women on gender roles which reflect these different employment-home relationships. Changes over time in women's participation in paid work, coupled with an erosion of men's former security in the role of worker, have contributed to the breaking down of the association of women wholly with the domestic sphere and men wholly with the sphere of paid work. Data discussed elsewhere (Pilcher 1994) on the middle cohort of women's accounts of men's participation in housework showed they were considerably more accepting of men doing housework than were the oldest cohort. Data on these women's own domestic arrangements at the time of the interviews showed them retaining responsibility for domestic work, despite significant levels of engagement in paid work. Some women, consequently, spoke of their often inequitable domestic arrangements as a 'bone of contention' between themselves and their husbands, and there were reports of efforts to increase their husbands' input (see also Brannen and Moss 1991). Accounts of men doing housework given by the youngest cohort showed that, particularly when they spoke of their anticipated domestic arrangements, these women were emphatically supportive of the involvement of men in housework. Frequently, it was men not doing housework that was an issue and they held high expectations of men's participation in the domestic sphere. For the younger cohorts of women, therefore, gender did not excuse the participation of men in housework. Nor did gender preclude the participation of women in paid work, including as 'breadwinner'. Therefore, in their accounts, role reversal was largely constructed as an issue of practicality: the gender of who does what was immaterial.

Whilst over time, women's changed relationship to paid work may have contributed to the erosion of the relevance and acceptability of traditional vocabularies of gender roles and responsibilities, other 'vocabularies of motive' have gained greater hold. Individualist ideologies, comprising (amongst other elements) a belief in autonomy and the free action of individuals, have become an increasingly prominent feature of Western industrial society and an increasingly acceptable 'vocabulary of motive'. (Lukes 1973; Hutson and Jenkins 1989). Equality and structural constraints vocabularies were rarely employed in the accounts of role reversal, but where they were, it was mostly by women of the youngest cohort. Arguably, this is a reflection of their greater exposure to egalitarian and feminist ideologies which have made systemic and systematic gender inequality a focus of concern. In contrast to the emphasis on individual choice contained within individualism, the equality and structural constraints vocabularies suggest a recognition of restricted opportunities *collectively* faced by people, especially women, on the basis of gender. Contrasting experiences of and exposure to traditional gender roles and practices, and to the ideologies of individualism and feminism are suggested, then, as aspects of the differing gendered opportunity structures faced by the three cohorts of women, which are reflected in the vocabulary they used to talk about role reversal.

3. A man's world? Accounts of equality and discrimination

The inequalities and discrimination experienced by women in the 'public' world, of paid work and politics for example, have been on the agenda of the feminist movement from its very inception in the mid to late nineteenth century. The notion of equality is central to liberal philosophies and, whatever feminism is taken to propose, the equality of women with men must be recognised as its fundamental principle. At its root, the feminist principle of equality contends that women have 'equal worth' with men. From this emphasis on an 'equality of value' derive claims for an 'equality of rights' with men (Charvet 1982). Equality between men and women is taken to be a basic human or individual right and, therefore, inequalities and discrimination faced by women are regarded as pernicious violations of their human value. A second position on the issue of equality also accepts the equal human value or individual worth of women and men but maintains that there are fundamental differences between them. 'Thus are justified the separate and traditional spheres of men and women, by which the public worlds of economic and political society with their appropriate rights are reserved for men, and women are directed to the household and the family' (Charvet 1982: 1). Although present throughout the twentieth century, this ideology was particularly resurgent after the ending of the two world wars (Braybon and Summerfield 1987; Beddoe 1989). Contemporary proponents of this position are represented by, amongst others, the 'Campaign for Family and Womanhood' or the 'Campaign for the Feminine Woman' (Campaign for Family and Womanhood 1988-9). This perspective on equality regards formal equality between men and women as being inappropriate and unnatural; discrimination and inequalities of opportunity are therefore tolerated and even advocated.

Since the beginning of the twentieth century, the idea that women's equal worth with men should translate into equal rights with men has held sway, for there has been a gradual extension of legislation formally providing for equality between women and men. This body of legislation has encouraged some commentators to describe contemporary Britain as a 'post-feminist society' and to deny the relevance of gender as a basis for discrimination. However, sociological evidence, including that documented by the Equal Opportunities Commission, suggests the contrary: women, in particular, continue to be disadvantaged compared to men. Irrespective of the prevalence of gender inequality in contemporary Britain, few would deny that marked changes have occurred during the twentieth century in women's status in the 'public' sphere and that legislation has made an important contribution via establishing the principle of equal rights for women and men.

As a consequence of the legislation-based changes in women's status and position in the public sphere, the three cohorts of women in this study are likely to have faced contrasting 'gendered opportunity structures' (Walby 1997), in terms of formal access to types and levels of paid work, education and a whole range of services. For this reason, the topic of 'equality' between women and men in society was an important one for exploring the ways in which cohort acts upon the construction of gender issues. The first part of this chapter outlines a socio-historical context in which to locate the women's accounts of the nature and extent of gender equality. Differences between the cohorts of women in terms of whether equality or inequality and discrimination was said to predominate in contemporary Britain are considered next, whilst the main part of the chapter examines the ranges of ways the women talked about these issues.

Equality, legislation and social change

According to Banks (1981), the most important strand of nineteenth century feminism was 'equal rights' feminism: its central concerns were the legal rights of married women, issues of the employment of women and the suffrage question. The suffrage question was partly settled in 1918, when the *Representation of the People Act* allowed women over the age of 30 to vote (if they were a householder or the wife of a local government elector), together with all men aged over 21. Another decade passed before women won the vote on equal terms with men, with the 1928 *Equal Franchise Act*. In the field of employment, an early important piece of legislation was the 1919 *Sex Disqualification (Removal) Act*. This stated that neither sex nor marriage should disqualify anyone from public or civil appointments or professions. Dyhouse (1989), however, describes the legislation as 'wholly ineffectual' and documents how, subsequent to the Act, a marriage bar operated in both public and private industry, and indeed continued to do so throughout the interwar years (Hunt 1988). The Second World War saw women encouraged and later, obliged, to enter the formal world of work, especially in jobs that had traditionally been seen as 'men's jobs'. However, as had occurred after World War One, at the cessation of hostilities women were encouraged back into the home in order to leave such jobs for the returning servicemen (Braybon and Summerfield 1987; Beddoe 1989).

Significant formal changes to the promotion of equality and prevention of discrimination in the public arena did not occur until the 1970s. The 1970 *Equal Pay Act* (and its 1984 amendment) requires employers to give 'equal treatment' for pay, terms and conditions of employment to men and women working in the same plant, who are employed on 'like work' (i.e. 'of the same or broadly similar nature'), or who are employed on work which, though different, has been given an 'equal value' under a job evaluation scheme (Snell 1986). The 1975 *Sex Discrimination Act* made it illegal to discriminate on the grounds of sex in employment, education and the provision of services. The Equal Opportunities Commission was set up to oversee the workings of the Act. Also passed in 1975 was the *Employment Protection Act*, which made it unlawful to dismiss a woman due to pregnancy. It established the right to maternity leave, maternity pay and the right to return to the job. In 1986, the *Sex Discrimination Act* was amended so that workplaces of five or less employees were no longer exempt from the terms of the legislation. In many respects, such legislation has been limited in its effectiveness; procedurally, it is difficult to take a case through the tribunal system, and to win it (Leonard 1987), and many women remain ignorant of their rights under the various pieces of legislation. Research by Collinson *et al* (1990) has revealed the variety of practices through which employers and recruiters still 'manage to discriminate' against women. Consequently, forms and types of paid work remain highly gendered and women working full-time continue to earn only 72% of men's average full-time weekly wages. Despite its limited success, survey data show high levels of public support for equal opportunities legislation. The 1987 *British Social Attitudes* survey found that 75% of respondents supported the law against sex discrimination (Witherspoon 1988). These data also suggest that the feminist principle of equal rights on the grounds of equal value holds sway in public opinion over the view that, although of equal worth, women and men are fundamentally different, requiring different roles, rights and opportunities.

Equality now?

In this study, data on issues of equality and discrimination are drawn from responses to a series of questions, concerned with whether or not men and women enjoy the 'same chances', have 'equal opportunities' and get 'treated equally' in contemporary society. The basic findings (in numerical terms) are shown in Table Two. A majority of the sample overall gave accounts which suggested that equality had been achieved. However, the data showed marked differences by cohort. The majority of the oldest cohort (15) gave accounts which suggested that equality between women and men had been achieved. In contrast, the majority of the middle cohort (13) gave accounts which suggested that equality had not been achieved. The youngest cohort were the most equivocal in their accounts of the attainment of equality.

Table 2   **Accounts of the Attainment of Equality**

	Oldest Cohort	Middle Cohort	Youngest Cohort	TOTAL
Achieved	15	6	10	31
Not Achieved	2	13	9	24
No data	2	-	-	2
TOTAL	19	19	19	57

In reaching their conclusions about whether or not equality had been achieved between men and women, the women drew mostly upon their general knowledge, gained from the media and from public debate. Few women recognised that they themselves had ever directly experienced unequal treatment or discrimination on the grounds of being a woman.

Survey data on public perceptions of continued inequalities between men and women are available from *British Social Attitudes*. In 1987, 44% of respondents said that it happened 'a lot' that women are less likely to be promoted than similarly qualified men, and 37% said that it happened 'a little'. Around 54% of respondents said that job opportunities were generally worse for women (Witherspoon 1988). On the basis of the survey evidence, it would seem that the oldest cohort of women in this study were out of step with the generally held view, whilst the accounts of the younger cohorts were more in line.

The qualitative analysis of the women's responses to the series of questions on equality and discrimination led to the identification of three distinct ways they talked about these issues. These are first, *a vocabulary of equality* which conveyed a recognition that equality had been achieved, and thus either explicitly or implicitly constructed equality as 'good'. Second, a *vocabulary of inequality* which acknowledged inequality and contained descriptions of discrimination. Such a vocabulary amounts to one in which, either explicitly or implicitly, equality between men and women is posited as 'good' and inequality and discrimination as 'bad'. The third vocabulary set concerning issues of equality is *a vocabulary of essential difference*. Here, formal equality between men and women was not regarded as a 'good thing', whether it was seen to be achieved or not. In accounts where this vocabulary set appeared, such statements were explicitly made. Of the three vocabulary sets, the most prominent was that of equality, followed by the inequality vocabulary. Only a small minority made use of the vocabulary of essential difference between men and women. As shown below, there were important differences between the cohorts of women in the ways these vocabularies were used.

The oldest cohort: equality now

In terms of the attainment of equality, the majority of women in the oldest cohort gave accounts suggesting that it had wholly or mostly been achieved. Clearly, as suggested by the numerical analysis presented earlier, the vocabulary of equality was by far the most prominent way of talking about these issues amongst these women. Here, the women referred to equality having been achieved between men and women in a general and widespread manner.

> *[Do you think they (men and women) get treated equally?]*
> Oh I do, yes. I do. Over the last five or six years at least.
>
> Lillian Thomas, aged 75 (G1)

> Every way, every way. I mean, to me, the world is an oyster. Literally.
>
> Sybil Richards, aged 71 (G1)

> I think there are equal opportunities now for both men and women in different fields.
>
> Nancy Caswell, aged 69 (G1)

> Yes. I would say it's equal. Oh yes, I think it's better now.
>
> Doreen Owens, aged 70 (G1)

Opportunities in the fields of education and employment were most often cited as evidence of a general equality of opportunity between women and men.

Only a small number (two) of this cohort gave accounts which suggested that women in contemporary society mainly experience inequality and discrimination. In so doing, the women either inferred or explicitly stated that this was not an ideal situation. Their words are reproduced below.

> *[Do you think that men and women get the same chances in life as each other?]*

> Not according to what I hear on television...according to television, there are women who are not treated the same.
> Doris Ascote, aged 72 (G1)

> In some things. I mean, if a woman is doing a man's job, she sometimes doesn't get the wage that he is getting. So I don't think you can say that they are equal in everything.
> Dora Griffiths, aged 68 (G1)

Two women (Lillian Thomas, aged 75, G1 and Sybil Richards, aged 71, G1) gave examples of women not being allowed in 'men only' bars, but neither indicated that they thought such a practice wrong or inequitable. In fact, Lillian Thomas said that 'it doesn't matter because we [women] have got equally a nice place'.

A characteristic of both the vocabularies of equality and inequality was that 'equality' between women and men was regarded as a 'good', desirable state of affairs. Most often, this was implicit in what the oldest cohort said on issues of equality and discrimination, but there were examples of explicit statements. Some of these are presented below.

> I mean, I don't object to this equal status of men and women...equal status, that's great!
> Lillian Thomas, aged 75 (G1)

> [I]t was very wrong when it [equal opportunity] wasn't available.
> Rene Evans, aged 82 (G1)

> They [women] have good opportunities, which is a good thing, I think and I agree with it.
> Dorothy Powell, aged 79 (G1)

> I think they [women] should be treated equally.
> Doris Ascote, aged 72 (G1)

Three of the women quoted above made use of a vocabulary of equality and one (Doris Ascote), a vocabulary of inequality. Such explicit statements of equality as desirable and good contained within these two sets of vocabularies contrast markedly with the third vocabulary set made use of by this cohort of women. The vocabulary of essential difference was comprised of references to the impossibility and inappropriateness of men and women being formally equal, whether equality was seen to be achieved in contemporary society or not. Three women made use of such a vocabulary, all of whom also employed a vocabulary of equality. That is, they all gave accounts that in contemporary society, equality had wholly or mostly been achieved, but they regarded this achievement as a negative or inappropriate one.

> ...How can they [men and women] be equal? I mean, if God had made man and woman equal He would have made men have children, wouldn't He?...So how can you be equal? You can't. *[So you don't think men and women are equal?]* I don't think they are and I don't think they should be.
>
> Alice Nicholl, aged 78 (G1)

> *[Do you think that's (men and women being treated equally) a good thing?]*
> Yes. Some. *[Do you think men and women are equal?]* No. I don't.
>
> Ivy Keating, aged 87 (G1)

> *[Do you think they (men and women) should be treated equally?]*
> No. *[Why?]* Because it's inherent in a man, say, if you're on a bus, for a man to stand... It's in the man to be the helper.
>
> Edith Parry, aged 75 (G1)

The inference of the vocabulary of essential difference is that there are fixed and fundamental differences between men and women, differences which mean that men and women are not equal. Moreover, the vocabulary implies that inequality between men and women is a 'good' thing, arising from its 'God given', inherent or natural basis. Attempts at achieving formal equality of opportunity between men and women are therefore viewed as 'wrong' and inappropriate.

The middle cohort: still a man's world

In their accounts of equality and discrimination generally, the women of the middle cohort used the same three vocabulary sets as the oldest cohort. These were vocabularies of equality, of inequality and of essential difference. However, the majority of women of the middle cohort gave accounts which suggested that equality had not been achieved (13). Consequently, a vocabulary of inequality was most prominent in the accounts of this cohort. Only a small number of women made use of the vocabulary of essential difference.

In the vocabulary of inequality, the women referenced the non-attainment of equality and gave illustrations and examples of discrimination. The most frequently cited arena (nine cases) where women were described as experiencing inequality and discrimination was in employment, especially in terms of opportunities for promotion.

[Would you say that men and women are treated equally then?]
Well, I think men still get more preferential treatment. I suppose if a man and a woman go for a job and they have both got the same qualifications, the man has got the better chance. I suppose, because there is less chance of him giving up if he is pregnant or whatever (laughs).

Carol Mitchell, aged 38 (G2)

...I don't think you get women who would get into a higher position. So there is a barrier still...// I don't think the men interview them to that stage where they can get into it. You get to a certain level and that's it.

Gwen Keating, aged 53 (G2)

...if a woman with the same qualifications as a man went [for a job], you can bet your sweet biffy that the man will get the job. I'm willing to bet on that.

Angharad Baker, aged 50 (G2)

I think, especially with a career, if you had a woman in a career, and...she went for an executive position, and so did a couple of men, I think she would be very lucky to get the post. I think they would give it to the man first...think there is still that stigma, especially in higher up jobs, you know, that a man *should* do it.

Susan Griffiths, aged 44 (G2)

There is an *expectation* within these women's accounts that, in matters of employment, women are invariably discriminated against. This expectation persisted despite their own reported lack of experience of discrimination in employment.

A second important area of discrimination cited by women of this cohort was 'men only' clubs or bars, and here several women did report their own experiences. For example, Rosemary Thomas (aged 46, G2) described sports clubs as 'the last bastion of the chauvinist male' and as 'really beyond'. She recounted how she was once in a club bar, at lunch time, and was asked to leave because 'ladies are not allowed in the bar before two o'clock'. Another woman reported a similar experience, and recalled walking in to a men only bar in a working men's club:

> Now, I *knew* it was a men's only bar, I couldn't go in there and sit and drink. But the fact that I was only walking round...and there was no way that they would allow me in there.
>
> Janice Caswell, aged 44 (G2)

Other women also cited examples of men only bars or clubs as illustrations of continuing discrimination against women:

> ...there are men only [clubs]. And you have only got to look at...the old fashioned clubs in London. Even some of the working men's clubs still practise a men only rule.
>
> Judith Ascote, aged 48 (G2)

> They have a men only club, it is just a club where men are allowed to go and have a drink. And I don't agree with that.
>
> Shirley Owens, aged 45 (G2)

> I mean, men have meetings, places, they go to where women aren't allowed...Political clubs have rooms, bars, snooker rooms where women aren't allowed. // Today, yes...women aren't allowed in. It's men only.
>
> Susan Griffiths, aged 44 (G2)

Most of those giving men only clubs as an example of discrimination against women made it clear how such discrimination made them feel. For example, Rosemary Thomas (aged 46, G2) described her experience as 'diabolical' and one which made her 'furious'. Janice Caswell's reported reaction was similarly angry and resentful:

> ...I wanted to blow the pub up! You know, I was so annoyed. I couldn't believe it.
>
> Janice Caswell aged 44 (G2)

Other women, however, were philosophical about the benefits of men only clubs. For example, Judith Ascote (aged 48, G2) argued that there is 'a place for separate clubs', for women as well as men. Others also reported having 'mixed feelings' about men only clubs:

> It annoys me, the fact that we can't go in there. But I don't object to them having a room, a place...I mean, most men swear when they are together. Which they wouldn't do in front of women.
>
> Susan Griffiths, aged 44 (G2)

> Well, sometimes I think it is a good thing. When they get heated and that, language-wise ...sometimes it's good and sometimes it's not.
>
> Joan Lestor, age 51 (G2)

For some then, not being allowed in bars or club rooms reserved for men accrues some positive benefits for women, because of men's perceived tendencies for 'anti-social behaviour' which women themselves are not seen to engage in (at least, according to these women's accounts - see also Delamont 1980).

In illustrating inequality between men and women, references were also made to the discriminatory treatment of women by the medical profession, the unequal treatment of women in pubs, women's vulnerability to sexual violence from men and discrimination against girls and women within the education system. Space does not permit an illustration of these examples of discrimination. Frequently, women of this cohort proposed that inequality and discrimination was a general, all pervasive phenomenon affecting women in all areas of their lives, as the following quotations illustrate:

> *[Do you think women get as good a chance in life as men?]*
> No.// I think any woman who gets anything today has just learned to fight harder. I don't think it's any easier. I mean,...they pay lip service to equal opportunities but it's not there...It's not in any area of society. They pay lip service to it.
>
> Cynthia Daniels, aged 53 (G2)

> *[So in what sort of ways don't women get the same freedoms?]*
> Well in certain job situations. Certainly in [sports] clubs (laughs). Generally in life.
> Rosemary Thomas, aged 46 (G2)

> Well...women should be allowed, you know *given* equal opportunities in all spheres, 'cause they certainly are not. It has improved but I still feel women have a long way to go.
> Pauline Evans, aged 39 (G2)

> *[Do you think men and women get treated equally in society?]*
> No. Even now.//...I think men still get - it is still a man's world. Definitely.
> Susan Griffiths, aged 44 (G2)

It is characteristic of the vocabulary of inequality, then, to suggest that the inequality between men and women in society is far from an ideal state of affairs and is something that should be rectified. Equality between men and women is thus implicitly proposed as a 'good', desirable and proper state of affairs, with the lack of equality proposed as 'bad' and deleterious.

The vocabulary of equality was used by six women of the middle cohort, and was comprised of references to equality as having been wholly or mostly achieved between men and women. For example,

> *[Do you think women and men have an equal chance to do things?]*
> Oh yes. Now they do. Yeah.
> Maureen Richards, aged 38 (G2)

> *[Nowadays, would you say that men and women get treated equally when it comes to jobs?]*
> Well, yes, I should think so.
> Brenda Jessop, aged 52 (G2)

For other women who made use of a vocabulary of equality, experiencing equal opportunities and equal chances with men was especially true for women with 'ability' or with education and qualifications.

> ...Women are getting a lot higher jobs. I think the jobs are there if they want to do them. I don't think there's any

discrimination...I would have thought that if you've got the qualifications it wouldn't matter.

Rita Parry, aged 42 (G2)

[Do you think there is equal opportunities today for men and women?]
Well, yeah. I think if you have got the ability, I think you have got really equal chances now.

Vera Nicholl, aged 56 (G2)

It is implicit within the vocabulary of equality that equality between men and women is a 'good', desirable and proper state of affairs and has largely been achieved in contemporary society.

As employed by the oldest cohort women, the vocabulary of essential difference contained forthright references to important and fundamental differences between men and women which were described as inherent, natural or God given. The striving for equality between men and women was seen as deleterious and, ultimately, an impossible and inappropriate aim. Oldest cohort women who made use of this vocabulary also employed a vocabulary of equality. In contrast, when women of the middle cohort used a vocabulary of essential difference, the idea of difference between men and women was expressed rather more subtlety and the vocabulary was, in each case, accompanied by a vocabulary of inequality.

Middle cohort women who used a vocabulary of essential difference expressed a concern with 'being treated like a woman', with the implication that equal opportunities or formalised equality threatens the continuation of such social practices. For example,

I don't believe in equality.//...I think men got [*sic*] their roles in life and women got theirs...I love to be treated - when he comes home with flowers. I like that. (laughs)

Susan Griffiths, aged 44 (G2)

... I wouldn't want to be treated equal to men. I would still like a man to open the door for me, which probably sounds stupid. And I think it's nice for men to give up their seat...I like to be treated as a woman. So I don't want to be equal to a man.[*Do you think women are equal to men?*] Not really, no.

Shirley Owens, aged 45 (G2)

Another woman also expressed a concern that increased opportunities for women had 'taken a little bit away as well':

> You used to get on a bus and you would never have to stand up. You'd go through the doors of the shops and you wouldn't have them slammed in your face like you do today. You very rarely see a boy walking on the outside of the road anymore, do you.
>
> Gwen Keating, aged 53 (G2)

Of the three women employing a vocabulary of essential difference, Gwen Keating was the most hostile to equality. She said that equal pay and equal status were:

> In a way...good for somebody who's going to manage the house on their own...But on the other hand I think it has given a different attitude whereas a woman can say "All right I'm as good as they are" ... I think that's been the whole trouble of it is this equal rights...Well, it's all stemmed from there. [*Do you not think that women should have equal rights?*] In a way, no.
>
> Gwen Keating, aged 53 (G2)

That these three women used a vocabulary of essential difference does not mean that they therefore proposed that inequality and discrimination were laudable states of affairs. This is underlined by the use of a vocabulary of inequality by all three women. To illustrate this point further, below are some quotations where their positions on the general issues of equality and discrimination are clearly stated:

> I think things are changing and there is more opportunity now than there was. And I think that is a good thing. And it should be.
>
> Shirley Owens, aged 45 (G2)

> The boy would have more pay than the girl, with exactly the same qualifications. [*Do you think that is right?*] No.
>
> Susan Griffiths, aged 44 (G2)

All of the women also gave examples of inequalities between men and women, including men only clubs (Shirley Owens and Susan Griffiths) and discrimination against women by employers (all three women). To a considerable extent then, these women employed competing vocabularies: one which presented inequality and discrimination as wrong and deleterious and the other which presented equality as endangering the continuation of social practices through which women's femininity is defined and constructed.

The youngest cohort: nearly equality, but not quite

In the accounts of the youngest cohort, there was an almost even divide between those saying that equality had not been achieved and those saying it had, with the latter having a majority of one. In their accounts of equality and discrimination, the women thus made use of the already familiar vocabularies, of equality and inequality. There were no clear examples of a vocabulary of essential difference.

As in the cases of the other two cohorts, the vocabulary of inequality was comprised of references to the non-attainment of equality, and included illustrations and instances of inequality and discrimination. A range of examples of inequality and discrimination were cited, including violence against women, men only bars, the sexual 'double standard' and 'male chauvinism'. For reasons of space only two of the most frequently cited examples will be illustrated here, these being discrimination in employment and inequalities in education.

Employment was the most frequently cited arena, as was the case in the accounts of the middle cohort (9 cases). For example, inequalities in types and levels of jobs held by women and men were cited:

[Would you say that nowadays women get the same freedom in life ...?]
No. I don't think so yet...generally there's a lot less women in jobs now than men, especially high powered jobs.

Eryl Thomas, aged 17 (G3)

[Would you say that women get as good a chance in life as men?]
Not really.// Men seem to get more jobs I think sometimes. Because, like doctors and things like that. There tends to be more men. There's women nurses and that but they're just sort of like help and that, you know.

Mandy Mitchell, aged 17 (G3)

It's nearly there. Not quite...it is improving. But not everything is equal.// Well, the men get the better jobs, the ones that earn more pay.

Kirsty Harvey, aged 19 (G3)

The expectation that women would be discriminated against when it comes to promotion was another prominent theme in these women's accounts of inequalities in employment:

> If you started off as a filing clerk, it was very hard to get anywhere else above your level, if you were a girl. Because they thought you would leave to have children...whereas if you were a boy, you would get up that much quicker.
> Alison Jessop, aged 24 (G3)

> It's very hard for a woman to get promoted to a manager or a boss. It's a lot easier for a man.
> Elaine Griffiths, aged 19 (G3)

> Promotion prospects aren't as good [for women] because they presume you are going to go off and have children.
> Isabel Ascote, aged 21 (G3)

The attitudes of men toward women in relation to employment and abilities within jobs also featured. For example:

> ...I suppose in attitudes men are slightly different to women, they still think they can do jobs better than women, they still think they are stronger and all that.
> Sharon Owens, aged 18 (G3)

> Like now, [where] my husband works...There is no women there. Because she'd be blown right out..// She'd be made the black sheep, type of thing. She's a woman, that would be it. She's a woman. She can't do the job.
> Donna Powell, aged 24 (G3)

The second main area of discrimination and inequality identified by the youngest cohort was education. References were made to the discouragement of girls studying non-traditional subjects and the unequal representation of women in higher education. For example:

> *[What about equal opportunities? Have they been achieved in schools and jobs?]*
> No, I don't think they have, not fully. You can just see really by the number of women that go into further education. I know it

is particular courses as well - in the sciences there aren't very many women present. I think there are still less opportunities and still discrimination.

Hayley Baker, aged 23 (G3)

[Do you think you have ever been discriminated against because you are a woman? At school, at work?]
I suppose you do at school. When you are in school, "you can't do that, you are a girl.."

Lorraine Morgan, aged 19 (G3)

[Do you think men and women and boys and girls get the same chances to do things?]
Yeah, I suppose so. But then again, more boys tend to get the university places. That has been proved, hasn't it. So no, they are not, are they.

Kirsty Harvey, aged 19 (G3)

As has been previously noted, it is a characteristic of the inequality vocabulary that equality is posited as 'good', an ideal to be aimed for, whilst inequality is posited as 'bad' and a situation that requires rectification. Often, this was implicit in the women's accounts. There were though several examples of the women explicitly stating their response to the inequality and discrimination they described as characterising gender relations within contemporary society. For example:

... in some jobs, you get a woman teaching a man, or she knows about the job. And then when they both apply for promotion, it is often the man that gets it. Which I think - that's terrible.

Elaine Griffiths, aged 19 (G3)

I totally disagree [with notions of 'men's jobs' and women's jobs].//[*Why?*] Well, why shouldn't we all be equal? That's what I think.

Kirsty Harvey, aged 19 (G3)

[Do you think there are equal opportunities?]
No. I think people make out there are equal opportunities to a certain extent. But I don't think there are total equal opportunities as there should be.

Karen Lestor, aged 29 (G3)

When employing a vocabulary of inequality then, the youngest cohort described inequality and discrimination as occurring in a range of circumstances and situations, but especially in employment and education. Whilst reactions to the described inequalities were often implicit, there were explicit statements describing inequality as deleterious and equality as something that 'should be'.

Within the vocabulary of equality, the beneficial nature of equality is also implied and equality is posited as 'good'. Around half of the women of the youngest cohort made use of this vocabulary. For example:

[Do you think there are equal opportunities in terms of getting jobs and promotion and things like that?]
Yes, I would say so. If you do the job, you get your promotion. If you are good at what you do.

Bethan Parry, aged 24 (G3)

Well, I think they are treated equal now in jobs. Yeah [there are equal opportunities].

Denise Nicholl, aged 27 (G3)

[Do you think women get as good a chance in life as men?]
Now, yes.[*In terms of jobs and opportunities to do things?*]
Definitely, now.

Rebecca Daniels, aged 29 (G3)

Equality as a 'good thing' was often merely implied in these accounts. In contrast, one woman made explicit her response to equality issues, through denying the relevance of issues of equality and discrimination to herself:

[Do you think there are equal opportunities?]
Yes, I would say so...// Yes I think so. It seems to be. It doesn't bother me.

Rhian Keating, aged 24 (G3)

This is an unusual example, involving as it does the denial of relevance of equality issues to the woman personally and by implication as a general issue of importance. To a considerable extent, most of the women's accounts of equality and discrimination suggested that these were issues of personal relevance, or of relevance because inequality and discrimination are deleterious in a general sense.

Conclusions

Analysis undertaken in this chapter showed that there were marked differences between the three cohorts of women in their views on the attainment of gender equality. The oldest cohort (with two exceptions) reported that equality had wholly or largely been achieved, whilst the middle cohort tended to report that inequality and discrimination are rife. The responses of the youngest cohort were rather more equivocal: nine reported that inequality was rife and ten reported that equality had been largely or wholly achieved. The qualitative analysis of accounts of equality and discrimination focused on the types of vocabulary used. Three types were identified: the equality vocabulary, the inequality vocabulary and the vocabulary of essential difference. Of these, the equality and inequality sets were most frequently used.

The *equality vocabulary* was used to report that, in contemporary Britain, women and men enjoy the same opportunities, chances and freedoms. It was especially made use of by women of the oldest cohort, but also by a significant minority of the youngest cohort. Within it, equality is either implicitly or explicitly regarded as 'good' and discrimination as 'bad'. The vocabulary suggests that gender is not now a determinant of opportunities or life chances. A *vocabulary of inequality* was used to report that women continue to suffer discrimination on the basis of their gender. It was especially made use of by the middle cohort, and to a lesser extent, by the youngest cohort. Compared to the equality vocabulary, it often contained detailed and lengthy descriptions or illustrations. Within it, equality is posited as 'good' and inequality as 'bad'. Gender is suggested as an important, if unacceptable, determinant of experiences and opportunities. The *vocabulary of essential difference* was found only in the accounts given by the oldest and middle cohorts of women. This vocabulary constructed equality between women and men as unnatural, or at the very least, detrimental to traditional gender power relationships. Inequalities were regarded as reflections of men's and women's differing natures, role and responsibilities and therefore as largely unproblematical. There were, however, differences between the oldest and middle cohorts in the way the vocabulary was employed. The oldest cohort tended to refer to God-given and/or inherent differences between men and women in their accounts of why they can not and should not be equal. Where the vocabulary was employed by the middle cohort, they referred to the social practices through which differences between women and men are maintained. Such practices, in their accounts, are under threat from the striving for gender equality. Within the vocabulary of essential difference, gender was constructed as an acceptable basis on which to determine an individual's opportunities and experiences.

All three cohorts made use of the equality and inequality vocabularies, although they did so to differing extents. The vocabulary of essential difference was not used at all by the youngest cohort. These differences can be interpreted through locating the women's accounts in the context of their life courses and cohort membership, which placed them in contrasting socio-historical structures. The oldest cohort had lived through many changes in the formal provision of equality, including, for some, women gaining the vote on equal terms with men in 1928. For these women then, opportunities available to women today must therefore seem very great and perceived to be little different from opportunities available to men. Consequently, the vocabulary of equality was a relevant and appropriate way of describing gender relations in contemporary public society. For some women, their understandings of the proper status and position of women relative to men led them to challenge the appropriateness of equality, via their use of the vocabulary of essential difference.

In the accounts of the younger cohorts, and especially the middle cohort, an inequality vocabulary was predominant. This finding can also be made sense of via locating these women's accounts within the broad context of their lives. The middle cohort were young women when the bulk of the equal opportunity legislation was debated and passed in to law. Inequalities and discrimination on the basis of gender were problematised during the early life courses of these women. Their experiences, in paid work, in social and leisure settings and more generally, may have further heightened their sensitivity to equality as an issue. Certainly, some of these women provided detailed and lengthy descriptions of inequality and gave examples of discrimination they themselves experienced. Several women of this cohort did employ competing vocabularies, making use of 'inequality' in combination with 'essential difference'. However, unlike in the accounts of the oldest cohort, outright disapproval of equality was less evident. The rather equivocal stance of the youngest cohort as to whether equality had been achieved or not may reflect both their exposure to feminist rhetoric on inequality and post-feminist arguments that gender equality has been achieved. Moreover, their stage in life course may not yet have provided them with the range of experiences reported by the middle cohort. This interpretation is supported by the citing of inequality within education contexts by the youngest cohort, an arena of their recent and often, current, experience. The cohort location of these women meant that a vocabulary of essential difference was not an available or appropriate way to talk about equality issues.

The women's accounts, on the whole, constructed gender equality as a 'good thing'. This finding indicates the hegemony of the idea of women's equal worth with men translating in to equal rights with men. However, in the previous chapter, analysis of accounts of role reversal suggested that the oldest cohort in particular regarded the domestic arena as the most appropriate place for women. There is a contradiction between this and their response that equality in the public sphere is a 'good thing' and has largely been achieved. There are also contradictions between the ways the middle and youngest cohorts constructed role reversal and their accounts of equality in the public sphere. When talking about role reversal, these women mostly used a vocabulary of individualism, stressing choice and preference, and thereby denied the categorical treatment of women and men on the basis of their gender. Vocabularies which stressed gender as a determinant of opportunity and choice (the equality and structural constraints vocabularies) were used only by a minority of middle and youngest cohort women. These contradictions suggest that, irrespective of cohort, equality is regarded as a more appropriate and relevant concept when applied to gender relations in the 'public' sphere of paid work than in 'private' sphere of family relationships.

4. A woman's right? Accounts of abortion

The right of an individual to bodily self-determination and integrity forms part of the liberal philosophical tradition in which feminism has its roots. If women are to have equality with men and participate as fully in society, they must have autonomy over their bodies, especially in terms of sexuality, conception, and pregnancy. Rather than their bodies being passive chambers for sex and for reproduction, women must have rights, choices and autonomous control. This includes the right not to have sex, the right to have heterosexual sex without fear of pregnancy, and the right to end an unplanned and unwanted pregnancy, via abortion. The feminist position on abortion can therefore be understood in terms of it being a 'pre-requisite for women's social equality' (Greenwood and Young 1976: 128). In the words of a pro-abortion activist:

> When we talk about women's rights, we can get all the rights in the world - the right to vote, the right to go to school - and none of them means a doggone thing if we don't own the flesh we stand in...if you can't control your own body, you can't control your future (quoted in Luker 1984: 97)

The issue of control over women's bodies is at the heart of a much wider struggle between women and men (Petchesky 1986), involving ideas about sexuality, family roles, the succession of generations, paternity and motherhood. In this context, abortion has been a key area of contestation and debate as gender relations have changed during the twentieth century. The legal status of abortion has altered quite significantly over a relatively short period of time, and there have been political campaigns both to extend and curtail the legal provision. For these reasons, the issue of abortion was an important one to raise in interviews with women, where the main aim was to explore cohort differences in the construction of gender issues. This chapter begins with a description of the changing legal and social contexts framing abortion in Britain in the twentieth century, which, as I go on to illustrate, shaped the women's responses to abortion as an issue and the ways in which they spoke about it.

Abortion, legislation and social change

The 1929 *Infant Life Preservation Act* ratified the accepted medical practice of performing an abortion only if this was necessary to preserve the life of the mother. The judgement in the *Rex v Bourne* case of 1938 (that the termination of a pregnancy was lawful to safeguard a woman's physical and mental health) led to a more liberal interpretation of the law and, by the 1960s, large numbers of legal, semi-legal and illegal abortions were taking place (Ferris 1967; Greenwood and Young 1976).

Women in this study, irrespective of their cohort, often used the phrase 'back-street' abortions to describe the ways in which women ended unwanted pregnancies in 'the past'. However, the richly descriptive and emotive vocabulary employed by the oldest cohort especially, contrasted sharply with the thin, almost matter of fact accounts of the 'same' past given by women in the youngest cohort. The oldest cohort said that abortion was known about via rumours, but heavily disapproved of: it was 'not spoken of' and was 'hushed up'. Public knowledge of abortion arose when 'something seriously [*sic*] happened' (Alice Nicholl, aged 78, G1), that is, when an abortion went wrong or when a prosecution for illegal abortion took place. Abortion in past times was constructed by these women as being both morally and physically dangerous. Emotive descriptions of abortion as 'shocking', 'terrible', 'dreadful' and 'awful' punctuated their accounts. Some told 'horror stories' of back-street abortions, which had often resulted in the death of the woman concerned. For these older women, abortion in the past was equated with danger, pain and death. The middle cohort similarly described abortion in 'the past' as something rarely spoken of or known about, but their vocabulary was less emotive than that used by the oldest cohort. Rather than being 'terrible' or 'dreadful', it was described as 'not the done thing' or as being something that was 'looked down upon'. Abortion was thus constructed as more socially unacceptable than morally unacceptable. Although some told 'horror stories' of back-street abortions that had gone wrong, more women of this cohort reported 'normal' stories of abortion, where the procedure had gone smoothly and was relatively unremarkable. Women of the youngest cohort constructed abortion in past times as something that was socially unacceptable: it was a 'huge taboo' (Lindsay Farrall, aged 20, G3). Unlike in the accounts of the older two cohorts, horror stories did not feature strongly in these women's constructions of the past (only one woman told such a story). Overall, their accounts of the past were comparatively sparse and unemotive and arguably reflected their distance from abortion as a mostly illegal, highly dangerous act.

Currently, the legal termination of a pregnancy is governed by the provisions of the 1967 *Abortion Act*. Under this legislation, a 'legally induced abortion' must be performed by a registered practitioner, in an approved establishment and certified by two medical practitioners as 'necessary' according to certain grounds. These are: risk to the life, health and mental health of the pregnant woman; risk to the physical or mental health of any existing child(ren) of the pregnant woman; risk that if the child were born it would suffer from serious mental or physical handicap (OPCS 1985: vii). The grounds for legal abortion are open to varied interpretation and consequently, there are marked variations in access to abortion regionally and according to an individual doctor's judgement (ONS 1997; Greenwood and Young 1976).

Feminist groups continue to campaign for abortion 'on demand' or 'on request', so that power over abortion would then reside with the woman concerned, rather than, as presently, in the (male dominated) medical profession. Opposed to feminist campaigns to widen access to abortion are anti-abortion pressure groups, such as Life. For such groups, abortion is an issue of morality. The artificial termination of pregnancy via abortion means ending the life of a foetus, which would otherwise be born and live. For 'pro-life' pressure groups, including the Roman Catholic church, the 'right to life' and 'the sanctity of life' are central (Greenwood and Young 1976; Rice 1971). Luker (1984) in a study of American pro-choice and pro-life abortion activists demonstrates that the two sides share very little common language. Those opposing abortion tend to refer to the embryo as an unborn child and thus, abortion as murder. Pro-abortionists argue that the embryo is not a child yet and belongs in a very different moral category. Therefore, language is politicised and a choice of words is a choice of sides (Luker 1984: 2, footnote).

Since 1968, several attempts have been made through parliamentary Private Members' Bills to change the terms of the Abortion Act; in particular to reduce the time period in which an abortion can be performed. Each attempt has been accompanied by renewed feminist campaigning in defence of the current provision. However, in 1990, MPs voted to reduce the normal limit for abortion from the 28th week to the 24th week of pregnancy (Knewstub and Linton 1990).

Changes in the legal provisions governing abortion have not taken place in a vacuum. Increased sexual liberalisation (which amongst other things, has led to the separation of sex from marriage), the problematising of men's violence towards women and their bodies, and especially, the wider range and increased availability of contraception (in particular, from the early 1960s, the pill), are all changes which, along with abortion provision, have contributed to transformations in gender relations, particularly in relation to women's autonomy over the own bodies. On the issue of abortion, equally important are developments in medical technologies. Advances in medical care have resulted in higher rates of survival for premature babies; under some circumstances, an foetus aborted toward the upper time limit may, as a consequence, have a chance of living. The introduction of the so-called abortion pill (the RU486) means that a surgical procedure is no longer always necessary in order for a pregnancy to be terminated. Abortion, as a result, may become more easily and more cheaply performed, and hence may become more widely available (Ferriman 1991).

Following the introduction of the 1967 Act, the incidence of legal abortion steadily increased, from 8.4 abortions per thousand resident women (all ages) in 1971, to 13.1 in 1991. In 1995, the rate had decreased slightly, to 12.0 per thousand resident women (ONS 1997). Legal abortion has become an increasingly 'normal' event, at least in terms of its frequency. Certainly, survey data suggest that public support for abortion has increased significantly in recent years. The *British Social Attitudes* surveys, for example, found that, in 1983, less than half the population was in favour of abortion for any of the 'reasons of preference' (including that of 'the woman on her own deciding that she does not wish to have the child'). By 1987, a majority of those surveyed were found to be in favour of abortion on grounds of preference. The surveys found that, in general, attitudes have 'shifted markedly towards greater acceptance of abortion' (Harding 1988: 41), including amongst Catholics and those aged 55 and over.

A woman's right to choose?

Data presented in this chapter are drawn from a series of interview questions, the central one phrased *'What are your thoughts on abortion?'* The basic findings in numerical terms are shown in Table 3. A majority of the sample gave accounts which were categorised as 'sympathetic' to abortion. However, the data showed marked differences by cohort. The majority of the oldest cohort (12) gave accounts which were 'hostile' to abortion. In contrast, a majority in each of the younger cohorts gave sympathetic accounts.

Table 3   Accounts of Abortion

	Oldest Cohort	Middle Cohort	Youngest Cohort	TOTAL
'Hostile'	12	8	5	26
'Sympathetic'	7	11	14	32
TOTAL	19	19	19	57

Survey data on attitudes to abortion, contrasted by age group, show similar findings. In 1987, the *British Social Attitudes* survey showed that younger women aged 18-34 were more supportive of abortion, on all grounds specified in the survey, than were women who were aged 55 and over. For example, 57% of women aged 18-34 agreed that abortion should be allowed in cases where 'the woman decides on her own that she does not want the child', compared to 45% of women aged 55 and over. Abortion when there is 'a strong chance of a defect in the baby' was supported by 90% of the 18-34 year olds and 85% of the over 55's (Harding 1988: 49, table 3.3).

Qualitative analysis of the women's responses to the questions on abortion led to the identification of several distinct ways of talking about this issue. Two vocabulary sets specified the circumstances which may lead to the termination of a pregnancy. A *traumatic circumstances vocabulary* specified foetal abnormality, the health of the mother, or pregnancy as a result of a rape as circumstances which might lead to abortion. A *socio-economic circumstances vocabulary* referenced the age of the woman, her marital status, poverty, mothers who do not want any more children or irresponsibility in the use of contraceptives as circumstances which might lead to abortion. Three further vocabulary sets gave expression to the ideological rationale which framed both the particular circumstances vocabulary employed and the women's responses to abortion in general. A *vocabulary of individualism* emphasised that the decision on the termination of a pregnancy was 'up to' the woman herself. A *feminist vocabulary* also stressed that a woman herself should decide, but included references to a woman's 'right to choose' and/or to 'control her own body'. A *moral vocabulary* depicted abortion as a moral issue, either in terms of 'the sanctity of life' or of sexual immorality.

'Hostile' accounts

Twenty six accounts were categorised as 'hostile' on the issue of abortion. Nearly half (12) were given by women of the oldest cohort. Five of these women did not acknowledge any 'mitigating circumstances' which made abortion a tolerable event. For these women, abortion seemed wholly unacceptable, irrespective of the circumstances. For example:

> *[Do you agree with abortion?]*
> No, I don't! *[Not at all?]* Not really. I don't really agree. *[So if I said to you, should a woman have the right to one if she wants one, what would you say?]* Well, there you are. I don't know I'm sure. I don't think that I would [agree].
>
> Ivy Keating, aged 87 (G1)

> I think it's dreadful but what can I say. It's done. It's not something that I'd like to go on.
>
> Doreen Owens, aged 70 (G1)

In contrast, mitigating circumstances were allowed for by seven other women of this cohort and by all of the middle and youngest cohort. In the hostile accounts given by the three cohorts, abortion for 'traumatic' reasons was the most frequently employed circumstance vocabulary. For five women in the oldest cohort, exceptionally, abortion could be tolerated on traumatic grounds, specifically the abnormality of the foetus or the health of the pregnant woman. For example:

> Well, I don't like the sound of it [abortion] myself. I think it's awful...//...Well, if it [the foetus] was handicapped, I would say yes.
>
> Rose Jessop, aged 73 (G1)

> *[You yourself don't agree with abortion?]*
> Not willy-nilly, no...Medical reasons, if there is a medical reason.
>
> Sarah Mitchell, aged 64 (G1)

References to abortion under traumatic circumstances featured in six of the eight hostile accounts given by the middle cohort. In making reference to such circumstances, particularly the abnormality of the foetus, women used a vocabulary of abortion which is widely available in society, not least because such circumstances are embodied in the current abortion legislation. For example:

[What are your thoughts on abortion?]
No, I don't really agree with it. Only in instances of health or...if the baby is deformed. I agree then.
Janet Morgan, aged 47 (G2)

Unless - the only time I do believe in it [abortion] is if there was something wrong with the baby...Or if the mother's life is at risk...
Carol Mitchell, aged 38 (G2)

There were two examples of a traumatic circumstances vocabulary in the five hostile accounts of the youngest cohort, one specifying 'medical grounds' (Karen Lestor, aged 29, G3) and one where the pregnancy was the result of a rape:

It depends on the circumstances. I mean, if you were raped and you got pregnant, you wouldn't want to have that child, would you?...
Elaine Griffiths, aged 19 (G3)

Across the cohorts, traumatic circumstances, particularly foetal abnormality, appeared to provide grounds for the termination of a pregnancy, even for those who were otherwise opposed to abortion. This finding is in line with survey data, which suggests that even amongst women aged 55 and over, 85% agreed with abortion when there is a strong chance of a defect in a baby (Harding 1988). Only women in the youngest cohort mentioned a rape pregnancy as a traumatic circumstance which made abortion an appropriate choice (as shown below, it was also mentioned in their sympathetic accounts).

A vocabulary of socio-economic circumstances was also used in the hostile accounts given by all three cohorts to indicate grounds on which an abortion might be tolerated. It was used by four women in the oldest cohort, who conveyed an especial concern over 'unwanted children':

[What do you think about abortions, yourself?]
Me? I wouldn't have one. (laughs) I think it's awful. I don't like abortions...I mean, it is not fair to see someone bringing up a baby that they don't want.
Dora Griffiths, aged 68 (G1)

> I don't really thinks its good...but if they don't want the baby, that's the only way...
>
> Yvonne Daniels, aged 75 (G1)

One woman said that, although abortion may be tolerated for health reasons and even for a mother who wants no more children, it was inappropriate for younger (and by implication, unmarried) women:

> But I don't believe in youngsters having abortions. I am really dead against it... I don't think it's right for the girls.
>
> Sybil Richards, aged 71 (G1)

In direct contrast, for Karen Lestor (aged 29, G3), 'schoolgirls' were part of a 'very small minority of people' for whom abortion is 'a good thing'. Some in the middle cohort also identified 'types' of women when specifying socio-economic circumstances for abortion. Miriam Powell (aged 43, G2) specified, presumably out of a concern for the future welfare of a child born to such women, that 'prostitutes' or 'career women' should have the right to an abortion on demand but not other women. Concern for the welfare of an unwanted child also featured in the hostile account of another in this cohort:

> I still don't believe in it [abortion], I don't agree with it anyway. Then again,...I wouldn't want a child brought in to the world unloved and unwanted.
>
> Gwen Keating, aged 53 (G2)

A further feature of the socio-economic circumstances vocabulary were references to the ready availability of contraceptives for sexually active women. As Sarah Mitchell (aged, 64, G1) explained, 'I don't think there should be any need for them [abortions], with the birth control that's around'. Two women in each of the middle and youngest cohorts also expressed their disapproval of abortion in terms of the ready availablity of contraception:

> ...it is stupid of her to have got in to that situation [of being unintentionally pregnant] in the beginning, with the pill and God knows what, now.
>
> Angela Farrall, aged 44 (G2)

> I think it's wrong if you become pregnant and you abort, I think that is wrong. Because, you know, you are having sex so you should be taking responsibility [*sic*] of taking precautions.
>
> Elaine Griffiths, aged 19 (G3)

> ...I don't agree with abortion.//...I can't see why people get themselves in to that position when there's a lot more availability of things now...There's no need for it now...
>
> Rhian Keating, aged 24 (G3)

For these women, having an abortion without extenuating traumatic circumstances is unnecessary and inappropriate, especially since women 'now' are more able to control their fertility through the prevention of pregnancy. This concern also featured in accounts sympathetic to abortion, as shown below.

In addition to vocabularies which specified 'mitigating circumstances' for abortion, present in the hostile accounts given by the women were vocabularies which gave expression to 'ideological rationales'. Here, a moral vocabulary, with references to the 'sanctity of life', was especially to the fore. Four women of the oldest cohort and three women in the middle cohort expressed their hostility to abortion in this way. For example:

> Well, I don't like it [abortion] myself. *[Do you think that women should have the right to an abortion if they want one?]* No, because they are destroying life, aren't they.
>
> Hetty Morgan, aged 85 (G1)

> ...I would personally never agree with it. Because I think it's murder...//...I mean, it appals me, the lateness of the thing [in terms of the length of the pregnancy]. Well, I think that's absolutely criminal...
>
> Rosemary Thomas, aged 46 (G2)

> Nobody I knew ever had abortions...They would have been classed as murderers, as far as I'm concerned...// ...Every person has got a right to life. An unborn child is a life.
>
> Susan Griffiths, aged 44 (G2)

Two women of the youngest cohort also used this vocabulary, describing abortion as 'killing' and as 'disgusting'. The vocabulary is widely available in society, since it features strongly in the campaigns of the various pressure groups that have the curtailment or prohibition of abortion as their aim.

References to abortion as being equivalent to murder, and to 'the right to life' are core features of anti-abortion discourse. Moreover, the vocabulary includes much of the Catholic church's teaching on matters of fertility and reproduction. However, only one women made a direct reference to religious principles or influences as part of her hostile account of abortion:

> Well, I don't believe in it [abortion] personally. That's against my religion [Roman Catholic]... //...I don't see that anyone has got the right to take another life...
>
> Carol Mitchell, aged 38 (G2)

Within the moral vocabulary as used by the oldest cohort, abortion was also set within the context of sexual morality. It demonstrated a concern with the links between the availability of abortion and sexual activities, particularly of young women:

> *[Should women have the right to an abortion, regardless of the circumstances?]*
> Regardless of the circumstances, ah yes. I would think that she was very promiscuous, you see, regardless of any situation.
>
> Sarah Mitchell, aged 64 (G1)

> ...I don't believe in youngsters having abortions. I am really dead against it. For the simple reason, for them...it is just another thing. They don't take it seriously enough...
>
> Sybil Richards, aged 71 (G1)

This form of the moral vocabulary was only used by the oldest cohort. For these women, given their socialisation and historical experiences, pre-marital sexual activity would be associated with unplanned pregnancies and would generally be deemed 'inappropriate'. Freely available abortion might then be interpreted as reducing the curtailment of pre-marital sexual activity through the risk of unplanned pregnancy.

Where the women themselves had not said whether or not abortion should be 'a woman's right', the question was put to them directly. Six of the twelve oldest cohort who gave hostile accounts of abortion, nevertheless agreed that a woman should have the right to an abortion, regardless of the circumstances, when this question was put to them (five did not agree). However, few went any further in their answer than merely stating their agreement and thus did not actively employ a feminist vocabulary of their own accord. The one exception was Nancy Caswell:

> *[Should a woman have the right to an abortion, regardless of the circumstances?]*
> She's got the right, you know, it's her body and she is carrying the child, isn't she. So in that respect, yes, she has got the right to choose.*[But you wouldn't necessarily agree with the decision?]*. No, no.
>
> Nancy Caswell, aged 69 (G1)

Five women of the middle cohort who were otherwise hostile to abortion agreed, when asked, that women should have the right to an abortion if they so desired (three disagreed). None actively made use of a feminist vocabulary of their own account. However, one woman clearly showed that she was aware of the competing sets of vocabularies that surround abortion as an issue, including a feminist one which she disagreed with:

> *[How is {abortion} regarded today?]*
> I think there is mixed feelings about it. Some regard it as a woman's right over her own body, she says what goes on in her own body. Others still regard it as murder.//...*[So you wouldn't agree with those who say it is a woman's right to control her own body?]* No.
>
> Susan Griffiths, aged 44 (G2)

Of the five youngest cohort women who gave hostile accounts of abortion, two nevertheless agreed that a woman should have the right to an abortion if that was what she desired (three did not agree). The question led to one of them making use of a feminist vocabulary of abortion:

> I suppose she should have the right...it's your body, your choice. I don't think somebody should make that choice for you.
>
> Rhian Keating, aged 24 (G3)

The finding that some women agreed with a woman's right to abortion, in the face of their earlier expressed disapproval, is suggestive of the prevalence of individualism as a vocabulary of motive, particularly when an individual's 'rights' have been invoked. Agreement was expressed in individualistic terms, rather than in feminist terms, and was still posited as a decision that was disapproved of:

> Oh I think it's her decision, put it that way. It has to be. But I don't like it.
>
> Doreen Owens, aged 70 (G1)

> I think it is the woman's decision... It is a personal thing.
>
> Rosemary Thomas, aged 46 (G2)

> It is up to her.
>
> Angela Farrall, aged 44 (G2)

Overall, in hostile accounts, abortion was constructed as an action tolerable only on particular grounds, especially relating to the condition of the foetus. References were made to the sanctity of life and to abortion as killing and murder. Nevertheless, for some women in each cohort, their own hostility toward abortion did not prevent them from acknowledging that abortion should be an individual choice.

'Sympathetic' accounts

The majority (32) of the women's accounts were categorised as being sympathetic toward abortion, with the two younger cohorts giving the bulk of the sympathetic accounts. Only seven of the nineteen women in the oldest cohort gave sympathetic accounts. Six referenced socio-economic circumstances which for them made abortion especially acceptable. A concern was expressed for 'unwanted children' (three examples):

> Well...if the child is going to be born and not looked after...I think it's the best thing, for the child's point of view.
>
> Dorothy Powell, aged 79 (G1)

> *[So if I said to you, should a woman have the right to an abortion if she wants one?]*
> Yes. Sooner than maybe ruin a whole life-time and possibly two life-times...I think better an abortion, than a sort of half and half motherhood.
>
> Rene Evans, aged 82 (G1)

This form of the socio-economic vocabulary has a concern with the quality of life of children who are unwanted, as well as with the quality of motherhood for the woman concerned: abortion is regarded as a means of avoiding such a situation. No women in the middle cohort used this form of the socio-economic circumstances vocabulary in their sympathetic accounts of abortion, but concerns about 'unwanted children' were present in the sympathetic accounts given by the youngest cohort (three examples). Overall, seven women of this cohort used a vocabulary of socio-economic circumstances in their sympathetic accounts. Some cited the age and future prospects of the pregnant woman, probably reflecting their own stage in the life course:

> ...if it was a 15 or 16 year old and they didn't really want it...there is no point in ruining two lives, when one hasn't really begun.
>
> Ruth Richards, aged 17 (G3)

> Well, it depends whether they are still in full time education, whether they have got a career in front of them.
>
> Lorraine Morgan, aged 19 (G3)

Two women of the oldest cohort suggested that, with the availability of contraceptives to women today, ideally, unwanted pregnancies should be avoided in the first place:

> From what I can hear about this Pill, there's no need for it, there's no need to have an abortion...
>
> Edith Parry, aged 75 (G1)

This caveat also featured in the sympathetic accounts given by the younger cohorts of women. Two women of the middle cohort cautioned against abortion used as birth control:

> I don't think it should be available to people like it is in Russia...They just go along and have an abortion instead of using the Pill.
>
> Angharad Baker, aged 50 (G2)

> I think in some cases it is regarded as birth control, which I don't agree with. But I think it's a woman's right all the same.
>
> Judith Ascote, aged 48 (G2)

In comparison with the ways in which the oldest cohort used the vocabulary of socio-economic circumstances, these women were less concerned with the 'likely future' if unwanted pregnancies were to continue and more concerned that abortion, if available, is not abused and used as a form of birth control (see also Luker 1984). A similar concern was expressed in the sympathetic accounts of abortion given by the youngest cohort, where unwanted, unplanned pregnancies were suggested to be women's own 'fault' for having unprotected sex:

> ...with the number [*sic*] of birth control around these days, there is no *need* to get pregnant.
>
> Lindsay Farrall, aged 20 (G3)

> ...there is no excuse really today. Because there is so much contraception around.
>
> Wendy Caswell, aged 22 (G3)

For some women, across all cohorts, the greater availability of contraception meant that abortion should be largely unnecessary: unwanted children, premature pregnancy and damaged career prospects could all easily be guarded against by preventing conception in the first place. This concern, expressed through a vocabulary of socio-economic circumstances, was present in both hostile and sympathetic accounts. This finding suggests that abortion was recognised as a moral issue, even by those (mostly younger cohort) women who gave sympathetic accounts. Other data, on the awareness of moral ('right to life') vocabularies and expressions of concern over the timing of an abortion in terms of the length of a pregnancy (discussed below) also support this interpretation.

Ideological rationales were rarely evident in the sympathetic accounts given by the oldest cohort. Two women employed a vocabulary of individualism:

> ...I think it is up to the woman if she wants children.
>
> Alice Nicholl, aged 78 (G1)

> Well, I think if the situation is desperate, I wouldn't blame a woman who wanted an abortion...I wouldn't blame her at all.
>
> Lillian Thomas, aged 75 (G1)

This vocabulary emphasises abortion as an individual choice, to be made according to the circumstances. Lillian Thomas also went on to use a feminist vocabulary, in response to a question on women's rights to abortion:

> *[...Should a woman have the right to an abortion on demand if she wants one, regardless of the particular circumstances?]* Oh

yes! Of course she should have the right, it's her body, her life. Certainly I think she should have the choice.

Lillian Thomas, aged 75 (G1)

This vocabulary, with references to a woman's 'body' and 'choice' are central features of the feminist discourse of abortion. The six other women of the oldest cohort who gave sympathetic accounts of abortion also agreed that women should have the right to abortion on demand; however, unlike Lillian Thomas, they did not actively employ a feminist vocabulary in constructing their answer to this question.

In the eleven sympathetic accounts given by the middle cohort, vocabularies conveying an ideological rationale were more evident than vocabularies specifying circumstances for an abortion. In particular, women of the middle cohort made use of a feminist vocabulary. Six women expressed their sympathy for abortion through an active use of a feminist vocabulary. For example:

> I see it as part of the feminist movement that a woman should have control over her body...[that] she has the right to terminate the pregnancy.
>
> Pauline Evans, aged 39 (G2)

> I think that it [abortion] should be left entirely to the woman. I think it should be available on demand.
>
> Cynthia Daniels, aged 53 (G2)

> ...what *man* has the right to say that we shouldn't [have an abortion]? It's us, our body...I think you should choose to do exactly as you like.
>
> Janice Caswell, aged 44 (G2)

This feminist vocabulary, referencing 'choice' and control over women's own bodies, was also employed by three women of the youngest cohort. For example:

> I think it is a woman's choice, you know.//...I don't think anybody, anybody, has got the right to tell anyone else what they can do with their own bodies.
>
> Lindsay Farrall, aged 20 (G3)

Thus women in the youngest cohort used a feminist vocabulary more than the oldest, but less than the middle cohort. Furthermore, whilst around half of the youngest cohort showed an awareness of competing discourses on abortion, they showed a greater familiarity with the moral vocabulary of abortion as 'killing' and 'murder' than with the pro-abortion feminist vocabulary of 'choice' and 'control'.

A vocabulary of individualism, depicting a decision to have an abortion as being 'up to' the individual and according to the particular circumstances, was used by four women of the middle cohort and six women of the youngest cohort. For example:

> Well, that is another thing that is up to the individual.
> Joan Lestor, aged 51 (G2)

> I suppose it is down to the person in the end.
> Sharon Owens, aged 18 (G3)

> *[What are your thoughts on abortion?]*
> Fine. If you want it, have it.
> Bethan Parry, aged 24 (G3)

In sympathetic accounts of abortion, traumatic circumstances were mentioned in the context of overall support for abortion. For Janice Caswell (aged, 44, G2), if a foetus is deformed, 'there is no ifs and buts about' having an abortion. Circumstances relating to the condition of the foetus were cited by three women of the youngest cohort, whilst two others referred to rape pregnancies. For example:

> ...I am pro-abortion...like if somebody gets raped, I don't think they should have to go through the ordeal of having a baby, you know, from a stranger and from that experience.
> Hayley Baker, aged 23 (G3)

As noted earlier, it was only women in the youngest cohort who cited pregnancy as a result of rape as a ground for abortion. The youngest cohort may have regarded rape (or the fear of rape) as a highly pertinent issue, in the context of women's perceived vulnerability to sexual violence from men in contemporary society (Rose 1990). Evidence from the British Crime Survey suggests that, whilst rape is the fourth most worried about crime amongst women of all ages, it is the most worried about crime amongst women aged 16-29 (Central Statistical Office 1995).

Two women of the middle cohort who gave sympathetic accounts nevertheless expressed concerns over the appropriate timing of an abortion, in terms of the length of a pregnancy:

> ...I think the term is too long, they should cut it down, more than 20 weeks is much too long...The baby is formed. It could live.
>
> Rita Parry, aged 42 (G2)

> I suppose there has got to be a time limit to when you can abort. There is a time when a baby does become a person.
>
> Cynthia Daniels, aged 53 (G2)

One woman of the youngest cohort (Hayley Baker, aged 23, G3) gave a similar caveat relating to the timing of an abortion, saying that there must be an 'ultimate line' after which a pregnancy could not be terminated. This concern was also found to be of importance to pro-choice activists in Luker's (1984) study and is described as a 'gradualist position'. That is, that the problematical status of abortion, even for those sympathetic toward it, increases the longer a pregnancy continues.

Overall, in sympathetic accounts, abortion was constructed as an acceptable action, and as a decision for an individual woman to take for herself and according to her circumstances. Nevertheless, for some women, especially in the context of freely available contraception, abortion was regarded as a option that should not be misused.

Conclusions

This chapter has reported on accounts of abortion and has illustrated the contrasting responses to the issue according to cohort. Women in the oldest cohort tended to give hostile accounts of abortion, mostly constructing it as a moral issue and especially in terms of the 'sanctity of life'. Women in the younger cohorts tended to give sympathetic accounts of abortion, constructing it as an issue of personal choice (especially the youngest cohort) or an issue of gender significance, via emphasis on a woman's choice (especially the middle cohort).

Qualitative analysis focused on the vocabularies used by the women in their accounts of abortion and the ways these varied by cohort. Two vocabularies sets were identified which specified the circumstances leading to the termination of a pregnancy. Across the cohorts, *traumatic circumstances* relating to the condition of the foetus and the health of the woman provided acceptable grounds for abortion, even for some in the oldest cohort who were the most hostile to abortion. Similarly, the women shared a vocabulary which portrayed abortion as an acceptable choice on *socio-economic grounds*. Especially for women in the oldest cohort giving sympathetic accounts, abortion was a way of avoiding 'unwanted children'. For women in the younger cohorts, however, including some who gave sympathetic accounts, abortion was regarded as an option that should not be misused, especially given the wide availability of contraceptives.

Three vocabularies were identified as giving expression to ideological rationales and here differences between the cohorts were more apparent. The most prominent in hostile accounts was the *moral vocabulary*, which especially included references to the 'right to life'. It was employed in an active way mostly by women in the oldest and middle cohorts (although, as noted above, women in the youngest cohort did indicate their familiarity with morality as a competing vocabulary of abortion). A *vocabulary of individualism* was a particularly important ideological rationale for the younger cohorts, especially the youngest, and was used as part of their sympathetic accounts of abortion. Within this vocabulary, gender seemed an unimportant issue: abortion was constructed as an issue of individual or personal choice. A *feminist vocabulary* was especially found in the sympathetic accounts given by women of the middle cohort. Here abortion was constructed as a gender issue, via references to a woman's body, choice, control and the necessity of abortion available on demand.

Women of all cohorts were asked, if they had not raised the issue themselves, whether a woman should have the right to an abortion. In response to this direct invoking of the notion of rights, even some oldest cohort women who gave hostile accounts, conceded their agreement. On one level, this finding suggests the hegemony of rights discourses as an acceptable vocabulary of motive, irrespective of cohort. However, few women of the oldest cohort actively employed an individualist vocabulary, not least in their hostile accounts. More significantly, abortion rights have been framed primarily in terms of gender via feminist campaigning, yet a feminist vocabulary barely featured in the responses of the oldest cohort to this question.

The differences in response to abortion by cohort and the variations in vocabularies employed when discussing the issue can be interpreted through placing the women's accounts in the context of their life courses and cohort membership. The reports of abortion in past times given by the oldest cohort indicated that abortion was morally and physically dangerous, subject to strong social disapproval and legal sanction. Unsurprisingly, then, their socio-historical experiences of abortion led many to be hostile to abortion, per se, despite it now being a legal and mainly safe intervention in a pregnancy. Using a moral vocabulary, conceding no mitigating circumstances for abortion or only under traumatic circumstances, were appropriate and acceptable ways of talking about abortion for most of these women. The finding that some women of this cohort did recognise 'unwanted children' as an acceptable ground for abortion is also in keeping with what is known about their likely socialisation experiences. Up until the 1960s, contraception was not readily available and 'unwanted children' were often the result. This cohort are likely to have been familiar with the pressures this placed on family life, making abortion a more acceptable choice on these grounds. In the same way, the women's socio-historical location via their life courses and cohort memberships meant that talking about abortion in terms of individual choice or as a 'woman's choice' were not appropriate or possibly even available vocabularies. In her study of women pro-life and pro-choice activists in America, Luker (1984) argues for the importance of education, class and occupational experience in terms of positions taken on abortion. Luker found that pro-life women tended to have made a commitment to the traditional female role of wife and mother, and as a consequence, were limited in the cultural resources (higher levels of education, higher class status, and more recent occupational experience) with which the pro-choice women were comparatively well endowed. Although analysis in terms of such influences falls outside the remit of the study reported here, Luker's points about investment in and commitment to the traditional female role can be applied in terms of cohort. That is, the oldest cohort women, found to give mainly hostile accounts of abortion, would have made a considerable commitment to the traditional female roles of wife and mother and, in so doing, had conformed to expectations that abounded during their earlier adult lives about the proper roles of women in society, including in terms of sexual morality and motherhood (see also Chapter Two, on their accounts of role reversal and the gendered division of labour). A further aspect of cohort membership affecting construction of abortion as an issue may be religious beliefs (Heath and Martin 1996) . Five of the oldest cohort reported that they were Roman Catholics, and this, in part, would account for the larger number of their accounts which were hostile to abortion and for their use of a moral vocabulary. In contrast, with Britain having become a more secular society, only two women in each of the middle and youngest cohorts claimed to be Roman Catholic.

The mainly sympathetic accounts of abortion given by the younger cohorts and their use of vocabularies of individualism and feminism also allows an interpretation in terms of cohort location in historical time. Vocabularies of abortion emphasising choice are likely to have been more available and permissible for the younger cohorts than for the oldest cohorts. In descriptions of abortion in 'the past' given by the younger cohorts, abortion was found to be less associated with moral and physical danger and more of a 'routine' event. For women in these younger cohorts, abortion has been legal and safe and is widely invoked as a 'right'.

Consequently, in their accounts, abortion tended to be constructed mainly as a question of an individual's choice, or an individual woman's choice. The feminist vocabulary was especially associated with the accounts of the middle cohort. These women may have been more exposed to feminist arguments for abortion on demand, arguments that have been a feature of campaigns defending the terms of the 1967 legislation. Luker (1984), writing of the American abortion campaigns, argues that the emergence in the 1960s of women as a self-conscious interest group, claiming abortion as a right, marked a new and fundamentally different stage in the abortion debate. In the case of Britain, Stella Browne argued for abortion as a woman's right in the 1930s (Greenwood and Young 1976) but the prominence of the language of control and rights probably did arise at the same time as Luker argues in the case of America. That is, along with the second wave of the women's movement in the 1960s and 1970s. Arguably, the middle cohort's greater use of a feminist vocabulary of abortion may reflect their socio-historical location in this respect. Stage in life course may also interact with cohort on this issue. The youngest cohort may have been less familiar with fertility issues as an arena of women's control and choice. Certainly, and unlike all of the middle cohort, most of the youngest cohort had not had children.

Contrasting experiences of the legality of abortion, set within a broader changes in sexual morality, and different exposures to moral, individualist and feminist ideologies through cohort membership are therefore suggested as aspects of the wider social context which is reflected in the women's responses to abortion and the vocabularies they used to talk about it.

5. 'Freaks' and 'normal people': Accounts of homosexuality

As noted in the previous chapter, sexual morality has been a key arena of social change in post-war British society. Marked shifts in sexual behaviour have occurred, including a reduction in the age of first sexual intercourse, an increase in the number of sexual partners, a greater toleration of homosexuality and the near universal acceptance of pre-marital sex. Such changes in sexual behaviour are argued to have taken place in the context of, for example, advances in control of fertility, changes in the moral climate and changes in the law (Wellings *et al* 1994).

An important aspect of the broad social context shaping trends in post-war sexual morality was the liberal left-leaning political milieu of the 1960s. Second-wave feminism was part of this milieu and had sexuality as a key concern. In feminist analyses, the 'sexual revolution' of the 1950s and 1960s did not fundamentally undermine men's 'ownership' of women's sexuality. Historically, women's right to bodily self determination and autonomy in sexuality has not been recognised, as evidenced by the use of chastity belts. Although this particular practice is a peculiarity of the past, a 'double standard' of sexuality is argued to prevail. Men's sexual desires and behaviour are privileged over women's through a range of social practices (including sexual harassment, wife-swapping, the use of women's bodies in advertising) which sustain the idea that women's sexuality belongs to men (Richardson 1993). From the 1960s onwards, critiques developed of heterosexuality as a patriarchal institution and the claim was made for women's right to define their own sexuality. Lesbianism was argued (by some) to be an alternative to patriarchal heterosexuality. In the radical feminist perspective, for example, heterosexuality for women amounts to collaboration with the enemy (men) and, consequently, feminist women should become 'political lesbians' or separatist feminists as a political challenge to patriarchy (Kitzinger 1987). In 1974, these shifts in ideology were reflected in two additions to the list of demands of the Women's Liberation Movement: the right to define one's sexuality and the end to discrimination against lesbians.

Whether from an individualist, liberal humanist perspective (Kitzinger 1987) or a radical feminist perspective, the idea that sexuality is a matter of 'choice' represents a marked contrast to 'traditional' sexual morality. Here, sex is equated with 'natural instincts' and biological reproduction. Emphasising the determining role of biology, traditional sexual morality constructs heterosexuality as natural and normal and homosexuality as unnatural and abnormal. Hence, homosexuals (whether women or men) are 'sick', 'perverted', or 'queer'. They are 'pathologised' (Kitzinger 1987). This essentialist discourse of sexuality (Weeks 1985) remains dominant in contemporary Britain. Survey evidence on the generally hostile nature of the public's attitudes toward homosexuality is provided by the *British Social Attitudes* surveys. These suggest that during the 1980s there was a 'steady increase' in censorious attitudes to homosexual relationships. In 1983, 62% of persons surveyed said that homosexual relationships were 'always' or 'mostly' wrong and by 1987, this percentage had increased to 74% (Harding 1988: 36). The survey question did not distinguish between male and female homosexuality. The term 'homosexual' was used in a generic sense; we therefore do not know whether the respondents were thinking only of male or of female homosexuality, or both. However, data provided by Wellings *et al* (1994) shows that respondents were less disapproving of female homosexuality than of male homosexuality.

Despite hostility toward homosexuality and the continued prevalence of the 'double standard' within heterosexuality, it is clear from survey data that sexual morality has undergone a marked degree of change in the post-war decades. Feminism has contributed to the changed sexual climate and particular strands of feminism have introduced new discourses of sexuality, including the right to sexual self-determination, the need for homosexuality to be of equal status and the emphasis on lesbianism as a political choice in a patriarchal society. For these reasons, homosexuality seemed an important issue to address in a study exploring cohort differences in the construction of gender issues. The pace and direction of social change in sexual morals and behaviour should be reflected in the women's responses to homosexuality and the vocabularies they used to talk about it. Before the women's accounts are examined, it is first necessary to summarise the main legal and social contexts framing homosexuality in Britain in the twentieth century.

Homosexuality, legislation and social change

Up until the post-war decades, sexual morality was dominated by Christian ideology which constructed sex as an evil, necessary for procreation. Sex was therefore tolerable only between men and women, and only within the confines of a marriage. Any other sexual behaviour was immoral and/or unnatural, including pre-marital sex and homosexuality. Ignorance, prudery and a gendered 'double standard' prevailed, which allowed men some sexual 'needs' but which constrained women to be sexually modest and pure. Homosexuality between men remained a criminal offence up until the late 1960s and so public scandal surrounded the discovery of an individual's homosexuality. There were also a 'series of sensational scandals' surrounding female homosexuality in the 1920s, which included an attempt to criminalise lesbianism and the banning of Radcliffe Hall's lesbian novel, *The Well of Loneliness* (Weeks 1989).

When asked how homosexuality was regarded in their earlier lives, some women in the oldest cohort replied that homosexuality belonged to a 'class of knowledge' (along with menstruation, prostitution and oral sex) that was not open for discussion. In general, the women of the oldest cohort said that they never 'heard' of homosexuality *per se* when they were younger, and several said specifically that they did not know what a lesbian was until they were well into adulthood. The very small number of women who offered descriptions of the way homosexuals were treated in the 'past' explained that they were social outcasts and subject to ridicule. Women of the middle cohort also tended to say that homosexuality was unheard of, or at least not spoken of openly, and that it was subject to social disapproval. The women of the youngest cohort tended to give accounts of homosexuality in the past which were more sympathetic to the ways in which homosexuals were reportedly treated. For example, Sharon Owens (aged 18, G3) said that homosexuality was regarded as an affliction in the past, and was medically treated. Others referred to the pressures which made homosexuals live secret lives and how this consequently must have been difficult for them. There appeared to be little difference between the women's descriptions of homosexuality in past times, apart from the tendency for the youngest cohort to give accounts of a more sympathetic nature. In comparison to abortion as an issue, the women seemed less able to construct a past when talking about homosexuality and this suggests that it may have been historically less pertinent an issue for these women. This may be due either to its lesser visibility in society, or its lesser direct relevance in the lives of these women.

As noted above, prior to the *1967 Sexual Offences Act* male homosexuality was illegal. The terms of the Act restrict homosexual activities (in England and Wales) to consenting adults which take place in private (Crane 1982; Warner 1983). In 1994, the age of consent for homosexuals was lowered from 21 to 18, following a vote in the House of Commons. The legislation is specifically concerned with homosexual relationships between men rather than between women. Lesbian relationships have never been recognised by legislative regulation of them, restrictive or otherwise (the exception here is in the case of members of the armed forces who are subject to the provisions of the Armed Services Acts - see Warner 1983). Whilst not wishing to conflate lesbianism with male homosexuality, the legalisation of homosexual activities in 1967 can be taken as a bench mark. The Act represented both a limited toleration of male homosexuality and a continued lack of recognition of female homosexuality.

Male homosexuality as a publicly contentious issue has re-emerged to prominence in recent years in association with AIDS and its perceived link with the male homosexual community (Weeks 1985). The extent to which there is a perceived association between lesbianism and AIDS is unclear but is arguably less strong than the link in the public consciousness between male homosexuality and AIDS. Other public controversies have arisen in relation to the various churches' dilemma over whether to recognise and allow male homosexual clergy (Schwarz and Sharratt 1990) and over Clause 28 of the *Local Government Act 1988,* which placed restrictions on local councils in terms of their 'promotion' of homosexuality (Thomas and Costigan 1990). The issue of female homosexuality gained greater visibility with the emergence of the Women's Liberation Movement in the late 1960s and the 1970s, via the demands for sexual self-determination and an end to discrimination against lesbians. Moreover, hostility to the movement was expressed through categorising women sympathetic to its general philosophy as lesbians (Kitzinger 1987; Holdsworth 1988). Accusations of lesbianism directed at feminist women are extensions of the anti-feminist philosophy that since feminists are 'anti-men' they must consequently be 'pro-women' including in terms of enjoying sexual relationships with them.

'Freaks' or 'normal people'?

Data in this chapter are drawn from a series of questions, the central one phrased *'What do you think about sexual relations between adults of the same sex?'*. The question did not include the term 'homosexuality' and consequently 'same sex' may have been interpreted to mean all homosexual relationships in a generic sense, or as only referring to male homosexuality or only to female homosexuality. The wording of the question led to some ambiguities in the women's accounts. Of the nineteen women in the oldest cohort, it remains unclear in eleven cases how 'same sex' was interpreted. In five cases it was interpreted as homosexual relationships in a generic sense (that is, they referred to both male and female same sex relationships in their account). In three cases, it was interpreted to mean same sex female relationships. In the nineteen accounts of the middle cohort, in eight cases it remains unclear as to how the term 'same sex' was interpreted. In five cases, however, both female and male same sex relationships were mentioned and in two further cases, male same sex relationships. In the accounts of the nineteen women of the youngest cohort, eight cases remain unclear but in three accounts both male and female same sex relationships were referred and in four others, same sex male relationships. In other words, the women did not equate 'same sex' as exclusively referring to male homosexuality. In the accounts of homosexuality that follow, references should thus be taken to refer to homosexuality *per se* (that is, to male homosexuality and lesbianism), except where clearly indicated otherwise by the women themselves.

The women's accounts of homosexuality were categorised into one of two categories: 'hostile' and 'sympathetic'. The basic findings are shown in Table Four. A majority of the sample gave accounts which were categorised as 'hostile' to homosexuality. However, the data showed notable differences by cohort. The women of the oldest cohort mostly gave 'hostile' accounts (14 out of 19). In contrast, 'sympathetic' accounts predominated amongst the middle and especially the youngest cohort.

Table 4   Accounts of Homosexuality

	Oldest Cohort	Middle Cohort	Youngest Cohort	TOTAL
'Hostile'	14	9	6	29
'Sympathetic'	5	10	13	28
TOTAL	19	19	19	57

In terms of overall patterns of hostility, the women were rather less disapproving of homosexuality than the general population. Half gave accounts which were categorised as hostile toward homosexuality compared to the three quarters of the population found to disapprove of this form of sexuality in the 1987 *British Social Attitudes* survey (Harding 1988). The survey also provided data on disapproval by broad age groups. In 1986, the survey found that 82% of women aged over fifty five said that homosexual relationships were 'always' or 'mostly' wrong, compared to 61% of women aged 35-54 and 59% of women aged 18-34 (Airey and Brook 1986: 166, table 9.4). Age was noted to be 'by far the most important discriminator' in terms of attitudes to homosexuality (Airey and Brook 1986: 153). As in the present study, younger women were found to be more tolerant of homosexuality than older women.

Qualitative analysis focused on the vocabulary sets used by the women in their accounts of homosexuality. Three distinct ways of talking about the issue were identified. Within the *pathological vocabulary,* homosexuality was constructed as an illness or disease caused by a mental or physical disorder. Those afflicted with the pathology were described as 'going against nature' and their consequent behaviour was categorised as repellent and abhorrent. A *vocabulary of individualism* emphasised that homosexuality was a matter for the individual concerned, especially if their behaviour (like other sexual behaviour) was undertaken in private rather than in public. Finally, a *social constructionist vocabulary* rejected the notion that sexuality is determined by nature or biology and posited sexuality as a preference or choice.

In order to establish whether women were familiar with feminist discourses on homosexuality, I asked a question phrased: *'Would you be able to understand a woman who said she was a lesbian for political reasons? Because she did not want to have anything to do with men on political grounds?'*. Few women seemed fully to recognise or understood what political lesbianism was, and fewer still were sympathetic toward it. Women of the youngest cohort more often recognised political lesbianism and seemed fully aware of what it represents. For example:

> ...that kind of woman I feel sorry for...Because you can't generalise [about men] like that...And I don't think you can use your sexuality as a political weapon.
>
> Lindsay Farrall, aged 20 (G3)

> Like an ultra, ultra feminist, you mean?
>
> Karen Lestor, aged 29 (G3)

The only woman whose account was in any sense positive about political lesbianism was a member of the youngest cohort:

> I think if a very radical feminist who just totally want[ed] to disregard a world with males and live - I suppose, if there are women who want to do that...then that's fair enough...I think it would be difficult like, if it wasn't a natural urge, just to do something for political reasons. But I can understand the statement.
>
> Hayley Baker, aged 23 (G3)

On the whole, political lesbianism was not a concept, notion or political stance with which many women were familiar and it did not seem to form a part of their vocabularies about homosexuality *per se* (however, homosexuality and specifically lesbianism, did feature in some women's accounts of feminism and feminists, see Chapter Seven). None of the women introduced the issue of political lesbianism, prior to my raising it. In contrast, Kitzinger (1987) found 'radical feminist' accounts to be one of the five types given by her informants (however, her participants were all drawn from an undergraduate population; two of the women quoted above talking about political lesbianism were recent or current students).

'Hostile' accounts

Twenty nine accounts were categorised as 'hostile' to homosexuality, with women of the oldest cohort giving the largest number (14). Five of these women did not use any distinctive vocabulary set to convey their disapproval of homosexuality. Like Rose Jessop (aged 73, G1) they often merely stated their disapproval: 'I'm definitely against that'. Similarly two women of the middle cohort bluntly stated their disapproval without making use of any distinctive vocabulary.

In the hostile accounts given by the three cohorts, a pathological vocabulary was most frequently employed. Eight of the fourteen hostile accounts given by the oldest cohort were comprised of a pathological vocabulary. Explicit references were made to 'nature', to 'instincts' and to 'abnormality'. For example:

> *[What do you think of sexual relations between adults of the same sex?]*
> Very much against it. It's against nature.
> Edith Parry, aged 75 (G1)

> I think God made man and woman, didn't he. He didn't make them for - oh, I think it's dreadful.
> Alice Nicholl, aged 78 (G1)

> It's abominable, because there are enough females and enough males to supply the natural instincts for sex of man and woman. But when it is a man and a man - or a woman, a lesbian - I can't understand it.
> Sybil Richards, aged 71 (G1)

Women who made use of a pathological vocabulary in their hostile accounts made reference to 'nature' and 'normality' to suggest that homosexuality is neither of these and thus should not be tolerated. Women using this vocabulary spoke emotively of homosexuality as being 'terrible', 'awful' or 'sickening'. For example:

> Oh, I don't like it at all...I think it is disgusting.
> Sarah Mitchell, aged 64 (G1)

> Oh, I think it's terrible.
> Doris Ascote, aged 72 (G1)

> I'm quite shocked about that. I can never get it into my head that it could be right at all.//...You see it on television, read it in the paper and I think, "Well, how awful!" I just am shocked at that...I don't like that sort of thing.
> Lillian Thomas, aged 75 (G1)

Accounts of homosexuality using terms such as 'disgusting' and 'sickening' also implicitly describe it as an abnormal and unnatural sexuality. It is described as 'awful' and 'shocking' *because* of its perceived abnormality. A pathological vocabulary was also an important way of talking about homosexuality within the hostile accounts of the middle cohort (four examples). Homosexual behaviour was again portrayed as repellent and abhorrent, due to its 'unnaturalness':

> (laughs) I don't like it. I find it sickening, well perhaps not sickening. Unnatural, that's the word.
> Susan Griffiths, aged 44 (G2)

> Horrible, totally horrible.//..it makes me sick. I mean, I don't know whether it should because it is obviously something they can't help.
> Vera Nicholl, aged 56 (G2)

> *[What do you think of sexual relations between adults of the same sex?]*
> The same sex? Not a lot. Well, it's just not natural is it. Not natural at all.
> Carol Mitchell, aged 38 (G2)

In Vera Nicholl's account (above), homosexuality is interpreted as an illness or disease that the afflicted individual has no control over. Here, sexuality is regarded as an expression of biological drives, and homosexuality as a unfortunate outcome of faulty biology. Women in the youngest cohort also used a pathological vocabulary in their hostile accounts of homosexuality (4 examples) and thereby conveyed their understanding of the 'naturalness' of heterosexuality and the 'unnaturalness' of homosexuality. An emotive language featured, expressing reaction to what was regarded as repellent, abhorrent, unnatural behaviour. For example:

> Oh God! (laughs) I think it is disgusting, it's horrible.
> Mandy Mitchell, aged 17 (G3)

> You are made a woman, and you are made a man, type of thing.
> You are not made to mix [with the same sex].
> Donna Powell, aged 24 (G3)

> I don't like it. But I think there are some that can't help it. They are born, sort of, in the wrong thing.
> Denise Nicholl, aged 27 (G3)

In the accounts of Denise Nicholl (quoted above), sexuality is constructed, not as a preference, but as something which an individual has no control over. Homosexuality is therefore an aberration caused by a physical or mental disorder.

A vocabulary of individualism was also used within hostile accounts. Two women of the oldest cohort expressed their disapproval of homosexuality, tempered by a vocabulary of individualism, saying "it's nothing to do with me and that's their business" (Doreen Owens, aged 70, G1) and "it's up to them if they want to be like that" (Yvonne Daniels, aged 75, G1). This vocabulary of individualism was more evident in the hostile accounts given by the middle cohort. Four out of their nine hostile accounts were partly or wholly expressed through a vocabulary of individualism. Such accounts contained explicit statements of disapproval softened by references to homosexuality being 'up to them'. For example:

> *[What are your thoughts on sexual relations between adults of the same sex?*
> I don't like it...But I mean, it's up to them. If they are happy together, then, you know.
> Miriam Powell, aged 43 (G2)

Not very good. No.//...I think if they're that way inclined, I don't think I'd like to stop them...As long as they keep themselves to themselves...

Gwen Keating, aged 53 (G2)

Well, I don't agree with it. But then you must live and let live, so.

Shirley Owens, aged 45 (G2)

Clearly, although these accounts contain explicit statements of disapproval of homosexual relationships, they also contain expressions of tolerance. Three of the six youngest cohort women giving hostile accounts also made reference to homosexuality being 'up to them'. For example, Alison Jessop (aged 24, G3) grimaced and said 'Urghh!' in response to a question on homosexual relationships, thus conveying her distaste of the issue. However, she went on to employ a vocabulary of individualism, saying that it is 'up to' the individual as long as she herself was personally unaffected by it. Other examples of a vocabulary of individualism employed in hostile accounts are presented below:

[What do you think about sexual relations between adults of the same sex?]
I don't agree with it.// I suppose I would accept it and I wouldn't condemn anyone for it.

Kirsty Harvey, aged 19 (G3)

It's up to them what they want to do, but not in public...

Mandy Mitchell, aged 17 (G3)

Overall, in hostile accounts, homosexuality was mostly constructed as repellent behaviour which goes against 'nature'. References were made to it being 'sickening' and 'horrible' and some women explicitly described it as an affliction caused by a physical or mental flaw. However, for women in each cohort, but particularly the middle and youngest, outright statements of hostility were often tempered by a vocabulary of individualism.

'Sympathetic' accounts

Twenty eight accounts were categorised as being 'sympathetic' towards homosexuality, with women of the oldest cohort giving the smallest number

(5). One of these women did not use any distinctive vocabulary. Having stated that she did not disapprove of homosexuality, she went on to say that:

> ...when you mix with them [homosexuals] you don't really know whether they are or not. It's only by either they tell you or somebody else tells you.
>
> Dorothy Powell, aged 79 (G1)

Within the sympathetic accounts given by the oldest cohort, a vocabulary of individualism was the most prominent (3 cases). For example, one woman told how there were 'a lot' of homosexuals in the place where she had worked:

> Well, I used to just accept it...I just accepted it as a way of life.
>
> Elsie Farrall, aged 74 (G1)

Two other women of the oldest cohort also made use of a vocabulary which can be recognised as individualist in character, one saying that a person's homosexuality was 'nothing to do' with her (Agnes Baker, aged 78, G1) and the other saying it 'is their business...their life' (Nora Lestor, aged 72, G1). The second distinctive vocabulary set present within the sympathetic accounts given by the oldest cohort was comprised of references to 'nature' and biology (the pathological vocabulary). Two women used this vocabulary, including one who also made use of a vocabulary of individualism:

> Well, it is a question of how they [homosexuals] are made. I mean, people seem to think that it's very disgusting and all the rest of it but then you get freaks in flowers, freaks of nature in the production of animals. Why shouldn't it happen? We are animals, virtually.
>
> Rene Evans, aged 82 (G1)

> If they are born that way. They can't help it, can they? If they are born that way.
>
> Agnes Baker, aged 78 (G1)

Thus the pathological vocabulary presents homosexuality not as a sexual preference but as the result of an abnormality over which homosexuals have no control. One woman of the youngest cohort also said that homosexuality was 'natural' to homosexuals, because 'they can't help it' (Wendy Caswell, aged 22, G3). No women of the middle cohort used a pathological vocabulary in their sympathetic accounts of homosexuality.

All of the sympathetic accounts of homosexuality given by the middle cohort (10) were expressed through a vocabulary of individualism. Again, reference was made to homosexuality being 'up to' those who engaged in it and as 'their life'. Some of the ten accounts comprised of a vocabulary of individualism had in common references to homosexuality 'between consenting adults', as embodied in the legislation regulating relationships between homosexual men:

> *[What do you think of sexual relations between adults of the same sex?]*
> Nothing much, you know...as long as you don't hurt other people. Between consenting adults...But no, I've got no strong feelings about them at all.
> Angharad Baker, aged 50 (G2)

> Between consenting adults, I don't see anything wrong with it at all. If that's their preference.
> Judith Ascote, aged 48 (G2)

> That's fine, as long as they don't affect anyone else by it.. I mean, as far as young people, when they don't know what they are doing or anything. But between consenting adults, I think it's fine.
> Janice Caswell, aged 44 (G2)

Two of the above quotations referred to homosexuals 'not hurting' other people, a concern which was a *caveat* in these otherwise sympathetic accounts. Indeed, such a concern was a notable feature of the middle cohorts' accounts. For example:

> *[What do you think of sexual relations between adults of the same sex?]*
> If that's what you want, I don't see anything wrong with it. As long as it is not forced on anybody who doesn't want it.
> Rita Parry, aged 42 (G2)

> ...Let other people do what they want to do. As long as it doesn't effect anyone else.
> Angela Farrall, aged 44 (G2)

Thirteen women of the youngest cohort gave accounts categorised as sympathetic toward homosexuality. Two were expressed without employing a distinct vocabulary. Thus both Rebecca Daniels (aged 29, G3) and Julie Evans (aged 21, G3) claimed to know men who were homosexual, which they did not 'mind' about or were not 'bothered' by. Most of the sympathetic accounts of homosexuality were expressed in terms of a vocabulary of individualism (11 examples). Thus they contained references to homosexuality being 'up to them' or to 'it taking all sorts':

> *[What are your thoughts on sexual relations between adults of the same sex?*
> ...I think it's perfectly acceptable, if that's what they want to do. It's up to them.
>
> Eryl Thomas, aged 17 (G3)

> Fine, if that's what they want. Let them get on with it.
>
> Bethan Parry, aged 24 (G3)

> ...I don't think anybody has got the right to tell anybody what they can and cannot do.
>
> Lindsay Farrall, aged 20 (G3)

One theme was that knowing (or becoming aware of) someone's homosexuality would not lead to changes in their relationship with that person:

> *[And what are your views on sexual relations between adults of the same sex?]*
> That's up to them. If I knew anybody that was, if I found out that one of my friends was, it wouldn't harm my relationship with them. I wouldn't shun them for what they were doing.
>
> Ruth Richards, aged 17 (G3)

> I wouldn't stop talking to them, just because they were.
>
> Bethan Parry, aged 24 (G3)

As with sympathetic vocabularies employed by the middle cohort, there were *caveats* contained within these women's accounts. These related to homosexuals 'not interfering' with other people and keeping 'themselves to themselves':

> They're just normal people when you get down to it. It's up to them if they want to be like that, as long as they don't interfere with anybody else's lives. As long as they keep to their own.
>
> Sharon Owens, aged 18 (G3)

> I'm not prejudiced against people like that...I think if they keep themselves to themselves. Which is the same with anyone. I mean, if a man pesters you, then he is wrong and I think it is the same then as well. If they keep to themselves, then, fair enough let them get on with it.
>
> Karen Lestor, aged 29 (G3)

> Well, it takes all sorts, I suppose...You have got to just accept it...//I think they should be discrete about it, really.
>
> Lorraine Morgan, aged 19 (G3)

References within the above quotations suggest that homosexuals are 'normal' people and that expectations of their behaviour should be bound by the same rules that should operate for heterosexuals.

Two of the youngest cohort expressed their sympathetic accounts of homosexuality in a vocabulary which I have described as social constructionist, in that it contained rejections of the notion that sexuality is determined by biology and nature:

> I don't disapprove at all. I don't think there is anything unnatural about it...It's wrong to say it doesn't bother me because I don't think it's right to distinguish. You are just discriminating against a different type of sexuality, then.
>
> Hayley Baker, aged 23 (G3)

> Fine, if they are happy...If you are happy with your partner, I don't care what sex it is, you know...It's only people's attitudes that make them have a different lifestyle.
>
> Isabel Ascote, aged 21 (G3)

Overall, in sympathetic accounts, homosexuality was constructed as behaviour that was 'up to' the individual. For women in the youngest cohort in particular, having knowledge of a person's sexuality was said to be of little personal consequence. However, for many women, homosexuality should not be 'flaunted', should be 'discrete' and should only be between 'consenting adults'.

Conclusions

Analyses undertaken in this chapter have revealed the importance of cohort in shaping responses to homosexuality and in influencing the ways in which women spoke about the issue. Women in the oldest cohort tended to give hostile accounts of homosexuality, mostly constructing it as 'repellent' and 'abhorrent' because of its 'unnaturalness'. Women in the middle cohort were rather more equivocal in their responses to homosexuality, with those giving 'sympathetic' accounts (10) having a majority of one over those giving 'hostile' accounts (9). Women in this cohort, whether hostile or sympathetic, mostly constructed homosexuality as a matter for the individual. The youngest cohort emerged as the most sympathetic toward homosexuality (13 out of 19), constructing it as being 'up to' the individual.

The women's responses to homosexuality were comprised of several distinct vocabulary sets. Across the cohorts, a pathological vocabulary was identifiable. This constructed homosexuality as an illness or disease caused by a physical or mental disorder and was especially made use of by the oldest cohort in their hostile accounts. Kitzinger (1987) reports on unfavourable accounts of lesbianism which correspond with the pathological vocabulary. One focused on lesbianism as a sexual activity and was characterised by an affective response of disgust and of personal discomfort with the whole topic of lesbianism. Kitzinger also identified an unfavourable account which posited lesbianism as 'unnatural', a description justified on 'religious' or 'scientific' grounds.

A second vocabulary set, individualism, was mainly found in sympathetic accounts and was especially made use of by the middle and youngest cohorts. Here, homosexuality was described as something that was 'up to' the individual, but also as something that should be kept private and discrete. It remains unclear whether, within the vocabulary of individualism, sexuality is constructed as a matter of preference rather than an outcome of biological drives. In other words, the suggestion may be that it is 'up to' the individual whether or not to follow their 'faulty' sexual 'instincts' or to deny them and thereby conform with 'natural' and 'normal' sexuality. One vocabulary set, labelled social constructionist, was only found in sympathetic accounts given by the youngest cohort. Within this vocabulary, homosexuality was constructed not as a pathology, but as a preference and a choice. The significance of a person's homosexuality was downplayed and it was suggested as an equally valid form of sexuality. In her research, Kitzinger (1987) identified what she called a 'liberal humanist' construction of lesbianism. This corresponds to the individualist and social constructionist vocabularies reported here, since references were made to lesbianism being 'a personal sexual preference for a particular lifestyle' (1987: 169). In general, the liberal humanist model was characterised by a philosophy of 'live and let live' and 'what you do in bed is your own business'. Both the vocabularies of individualism and social constructionism allow for the right of individuals to define their own sexuality and, with certain caveats regarding consent and privacy, also for homosexuals to be treated equally within society. To this extent, women in the middle and youngest cohorts can be argued to be favourable toward feminist discourses on sexuality. However, as noted earlier, this did not extend to an understanding nor acceptance of radical feminist ideas on political lesbianism.

A minority of women did not make use of any identifiable vocabulary set when reporting their hostile or sympathetic responses to homosexuality. In particular, five women in the oldest cohort who gave hostile accounts merely stated their disapproval. This finding suggests that the oldest cohort were reluctant to even talk about homosexuality: thus their accounts were brief and to the point. In fact, one woman explicitly stated her discomfort at discussing the issue: '...to be truthful, I don't like talking about it' (Yvonne Daniels, aged 75, G1). As the constructions of homosexuality in past times showed, for women in the oldest cohort, homosexuality belonged to a class of knowledge, along with prostitution, menstruation and pre-marital sex, that was not publicly discussed.

These differences in response to homosexuality by cohort, and the variations in vocabularies used to discuss the issue, can be made sense of through placing the women's accounts in the context of their life courses and cohort membership. Social history, as well as the women's own accounts, indicate that in the past sexuality per se, and homosexuality in particular, was strictly regulated and not available for public discussion. For the oldest cohort, homosexual activity has mostly been a criminal act and, more generally, belonged to a class of knowledge governed by Christian sexual morality. Showing a reluctance to speak about homosexuality or using a pathological vocabulary, which constructed homosexuality as 'unnatural', were therefore reflections of the women's socialisation experiences. For the same reason, speaking about homosexuality as a matter of choice, or constructing it as an insignificant issue of sexual preference, were neither acceptable nor appropriate vocabularies for these women.

The mainly sympathetic accounts of homosexuality given by the middle, and especially the youngest cohort, also suggests an interpretation in terms of socio-historical location. Women of the middle cohort were of an age to be exposed to aspects of the sexual revolution, which included the decriminalisation of male homosexuality in 1967, and the higher public profile of lesbianism in the context of the women's liberation movement.

Consequently, these women tended to make use of a vocabulary of individualism rather than a pathological vocabulary, even though a significant proportion gave hostile accounts. Women of the youngest cohort have grown to adulthood in a society where many sexual matters are openly discussed and where homosexuality has long been legal. For these women, speaking about homosexuality using a pathological vocabulary was less acceptable. Instead sexuality was posited as a matter of choice and one of little personal consequence to themselves. In short, within the accounts of homosexuality given by the three cohorts of women, it is possible to detect their contrasting socio-historical exposures. The wider social context which each cohort experienced in terms of dominant sexual morality, the legal status of homosexuality and the acceptability of individualism as a vocabulary of motive, have shaped responses to homosexuality as well as the language used in constructing these responses.

6. 'Just a bit of fun for the men'?: Accounts of Page Three

The increased sexual liberalisation of the post-war decades, which saw marked changes in sexual behaviour and morals, was also reflected in a reduction of legal controls over cultural representations of sexuality, including in the theatre, on film and television and in printed media. The relaxation of censorship, and the subsequent increase in explicitness and availability of sexual material has been interpreted in contrasting ways by various interest groups, including liberals, feminists and moral campaigners.

As with the sexual revolution' more generally, many feminists maintain that the reduction in censorship has not benefited women. The increased availability of sexually explicit materials may be welcomed on liberal-individualist grounds as an advance in freedom of expression, but feminists argue that the representations of sexuality which have subsequently proliferated are not gender neutral. In particular, pornography is argued to be damaging to women's status, because of the eroticisation of women's domination by men (Smart 1989; Jackson 1995). As Jackson and Scott explain, the feminist critique of pornography forms part of wider concerns about women's control over their bodies. 'It entails women's refusal to be reduced to their physical sexuality and resistance to our subordination as objects for male use and pleasure' (1996: 21). Moreover, as suggested by the phrase 'pornography is the theory, rape is the practice', in some feminist analyses, direct links are made between the availability of sexually explicit material and sexual violence by men against women. Right-wing moralists also regard the reduction in censorship and the subsequent proliferation of sexually explicit media as negative developments. For moralists, the increased availability of pornography is a telling indicator of the moral depravity of contemporary society. Its production and consumption is argued to be linked to the decline of religious influence in society, especially over sexual morality, which in turn has led to the separation of sex from procreation and thereby the erosion of marriage and the nuclear family.

Whilst there is agreement amongst liberals, feminists and moralists that the post-war decades have been characterised by an increase in cultural representations of sexuality, and that newer forms of technology have widened access, there is less consensus as to what sort of material constitutes pornography. Like beauty, pornography can be argued to be in the eye of the beholder. It is very difficult to define it in an absolute sense. This is one reason why two key pieces of legislation controlling pornography are, arguably, of limited effectiveness. The 1959 *Obscene Publications Act* is primarily concerned with whether or not the consumer of obscene material is likely to be depraved or corrupted by it. As Smart (1989) notes, this requires the formulation of a judgement on the meaning of the representation of the sexual act that is depicted, rather than the sexual act itself. The 1981 *Indecent Displays Act* aims to protect people from seeing images of sexuality that they do not want to see, for example, by restricting the positioning of pornographic magazines to the 'top shelf' in newsagents and by controlling the windows of 'sex shops'. Itzin (1992) notes that during the 1980s, prosecutions under the 1959 Act showed a consistent decrease, and only half of those prosecuted were convicted. She also notes that the 1981 Act has been used relatively little since it came into effect.

The problem of defining pornography has led to a shift in some feminist analyses. Increasingly, acknowledgement is given to the idea that words and images are subject to various and contrasting definitions according to context. This shift away from formulating a definition of pornography to a more nuanced, flexible interpretation is a key advance in feminist analyses of representations of women. It has encouraged a recognition of the 'pornographic genre' or a dominant style of representing women in cultural products (Coward 1987). One example of the pornographic genre is the way in which advertisements commonly use a 'pornographic' style in the depiction of women's bodies, via pose, facial expression and other signifiers of sexuality and/or submission. Another is the proliferation of the 'New Lads' magazines, such as *Loaded, Maxim* and *FHM*. These are not 'top shelf' pornographic magazines but nevertheless contain material which depicts women in a heavily sexualised manner (Landesman 1997). The only difference between such representations and those more usually recognised as pornographic is that a woman's sexual organs are not displayed to the same degree of explicitness (Smart 1989). For some feminists, the problem with media controlled by the *Obscene Publications Act* and the *Indecent Displays Act* is their explicit portrayal of women, sexually dominated by men and often in degrading and coercive circumstances. However, the legislation does restrict the availability and explicitness of such material, even if only partially. The problem with the pornographic genre is that it is not subject to regulation and control in the same way and consequently the public have free access and unrestricted exposure to it.

A long-standing example of the 'pornographic genre' is the publication of photographs of bare-chested women in daily tabloid newspapers. This practice is most closely associated with *The Sun* which introduced its 'Page Three' feature in November 1970 (Tunks and Hutchinson 1991*).* 'Page Three' is a daily photo-feature of a young, conventionally attractive woman whose pose endeavours to display her naked breasts to the best of her ability. The half-page photograph is accompanied by a short, jokey paragraph which provides some basic biographical details about the featured model; generally, her first name, age and hobbies. The feature tends to have a headline containing alliteration and/or a pun. It appears alongside general news items, of a more or less serious nature. In recent years, *The Sun* has faced some competition from fellow tabloid newspapers in the 'bare breast' market, mainly from *The Sunday Sport* and its daily equivalents. These newspapers have a proliferation of bare chested women throughout, leading commentators to talk of their 'nipple count'.

As Jackson (1995) notes, the inclusion of 'Page Three' and similar publications under the rubric of pornography is controversial. Yet in many ways, Page Three exemplifies arguments about the pervasiveness and pernicious influence of the pornographic genre. It is freely available to all, at a relatively low price and is made 'respectable' by its host, a national daily newspaper. Each day a new photograph is published and yesterday's placed in the dustbin or used to wrap chips, to clean shoes on or protect floors from muddy footprints or dripping paint. The objectification of women's bodies for daily, casual, cheap pleasure, as a distraction from the news, is then exacerbated by the disposability of the product (Jackson 1995).

Whether such representations of women in newspapers are degrading to women and have an effect on how men regard women has been a matter of general public debate in recent years. For example, Page Three has been the subject of discussion on day time television talk shows and of readers' surveys in magazines like *Woman* and *Cosmopolitan*. There have also been attempts to legislate against publications such as Page Three. In April 1988, Clare Short introduced the *Indecent Displays (Newspapers) Bill*, her second attempt to legislate on the matter. The Bill, which eventually failed to become law, aimed to ban the display of naked or partially naked women in sexually provocative poses in newspapers, making it a criminal offence, punishable by a fine, to do so. In proposing the Bill, Short said such pictures were degrading and could lead to rape and that the circulation of such pictures helped to create a culture which encouraged the sexual abuse of women and children (Johnson 1988). Short received over 5000 letters, mostly from women, who encouraged and applauded her legislative attempt to prohibit Page Three type publications. An edited volume of these letters was subsequently published (Tunks and Hutchinson 1991). An analysis of these letters shows that many made links between sexually provocative depictions of women and sexual violence against women. The question was also raised as to whether women really have a choice about being confronted with Page Three, in their workplaces and on public transport, for example. An examination of speeches made in opposition to Short's Bill (see Tunks and Hutchinson 1991) show the following to be central themes: questions of censorship; questions of the freedom of choice of those who 'read' Page Three and the models who pose for it; examples of public nudity elsewhere in society, such as statues and other works of art; and denials of any evidence linking Page Three type publications and sexual violence against women.

The widespread availability of Page Three, its status as a well known feature, and the public debate about it made it an ideal issue to raise in the interviews with women about gender. My belief that Page Three was a subject with which the women were likely to be familiar was confirmed by the fact that only three women claimed not to know what Page Three was (two in the oldest cohort and one in the middle cohort). Moreover, a number of women indicated their awareness that Page Three was a contentious issue, so much so that women who had never taken *The Sun* newspaper said they had heard of Page Three. In raising the issue of representations of women via questions on Page Three, I hoped to uncover contrasting responses by cohort which reflected the women's differing socio-historical locations, particularly in relation to their exposure to feminist arguments about the objectification of women's bodies.

'Just a bit of fun for the men'?

Data on the women's accounts of Page Three are drawn from responses to a series of questions, the first asking whether the women knew of Page Three and what they thought of it. A further question asked whether they believed Page Three had any effects on how men regard women generally. I categorised the women's accounts given in response to these questions as 'hostile' or 'sympathetic'. Central to this process of categorisation were the vocabularies with which the accounts were constructed, as well as clear statements of response and reports of any consequences of Page Three. Table Five illustrates the distribution of hostile and sympathetic accounts by cohort.

Table 5   Accounts of Page Three

	Oldest Cohort	Middle Cohort	Youngest Cohort	TOTAL
'Hostile'	10	7	8	25
'Sympathetic'	7	11	10	28
Don't Know	2	1	-	3
No Data	-	-	1	-
TOTAL	19	19	19	57

Overall, more women gave accounts sympathetic to Page Three than hostile, although the difference was not a marked one. In contrast, a reader survey by *Woman* magazine in August 1986 found that, of the more than 5000 women who replied, over 90% wanted Page Three to be banned. Also, four out of five believed that such pictures were linked to violent sexual crimes against women (cited in Tunks and Hutchinson 1991: 71, footnote). More nationally representative data is available from *British Social Attitudes*. Whilst not intending to imply that Page Three falls in to the category of pornography, the nearest question in the survey is that on pornography and is used for comparative purposes here. In the 1988 survey, 70% of women aged 55 and over said that pornographic magazines and films should be banned altogether compared to 39% of 35-54 year olds and 23% of 18-34 years olds (Harding 1988: 47, table 3.1). The survey showed that younger women were consistently the most 'liberal'.

In describing the women's accounts as 'sympathetic', I do not mean to imply that women giving them were uncategorically enthusiastic about Page Three. In fact, only one woman raved about it, saying 'I think it's great...I do...I don't think there is nothing wrong with it.' (Irene Harvey, aged 62, G1). In the accounts of other women which I categorised as sympathetic, there was often a suggestion that bearing one's breasts in a national newspaper was not a highly valued or particularly admirable activity. Thus, Janice Caswell (aged 44, G2) spoke of the Page Three models 'flaunting themselves' and Elaine Griffiths (aged 19, G3) of 'showing their bodies'. However, as shown below, there were clear differences between women giving hostile accounts and women giving sympathetic accounts in the consequences Page Three was said to have.

Qualitative analysis focused on the vocabularies present within the women's accounts. Four distinct ways of talking about the issue were identified. Within the *vocabulary of individualism*, Page Three was constructed as an example of freedom of expression either for the Page Three model herself or for the person looking at the photograph of the model. A second vocabulary set constructed Page Three as being of *little consequence*. Parallels were drawn with examples of public nudity elsewhere in society, especially 'topless' beaches. Page Three was characterised as 'harmless' fun for men and several women reported discussing the merits of particular models with men or reported their own admiration for the assets of Page Three models. A *feminist vocabulary* emphasised the negative effects of Page Three for women's status. Reference was made to women being treated as 'sex objects' and to the degrading nature of such publications. Some women also made links between the availability of publications like Page Three and sexual violence against women. Finally, a *moralist vocabulary* constructed Page Three as an affront to morality. It was described as 'not nice' and 'disgusting' and was said to have detrimental consequences for sexual morality, particularly in terms of prematurely awakening the interest of young boys in sexual matters.

'Hostile' accounts

Twenty five accounts were categorised as 'hostile' toward Page Three, with women of the oldest cohort giving the largest number (10). Across the three cohorts, hostile accounts were mostly comprised of moral and feminist vocabularies.

Six of the ten hostile accounts given by the oldest cohort featured a moral vocabulary, where Page Three was described as 'disgusting' or 'not nice':

> [It's] not nice for a woman to be in the paper and everyone gawping. No, I don't think it's nice.
>
> Agnes Baker, aged 78 (G1)

> Oh, that's those nudes...// Well, to me it is a bit disgusting really.
>
> Elsie Farrall, aged 74 (G1)

Page Three was also said to have consequences for women in terms of sexual morality:

> *[Do you think things like Page Three have an effect on the way men regard women?]*
> Yes, I do.// Well, sex and goodness knows what.
>
> Ivy Keating, aged 87 (G1)

One woman implied that Page Three prematurely awakened or intensified boys' interest in sex:

> They got to find out for themselves and that's what the trouble is.
>
> Elsie Farrall, aged 74 (G1)

These objections to Page Three are based on it being immoral or immodest in itself, and in terms of its consequences for awakening young boys' interest in sex, and interest in sex generally. The moralistic vocabulary was much less evident in the hostile accounts of the younger two cohorts. Two women of the middle cohort questioned the appropriateness of nudity in a newspaper:

> I don't think there is any need for it really, to have it in a newspaper... I think there is a place for that sort of thing, nudity, and I don't think it is in a daily newspaper.
>
> Shirley Owens, aged 45 (G2)

> I don't really see that's all that nice to sit and look through a paper and see that. And I don't like my son opening up the paper and seeing it. It's not so bad for men but for young boys growing up. I don't think it should be in the papers really.
>
> Carol Mitchell, aged 38 (G2)

The concerns expressed in these quotations allow for photographs of naked women, for men's enjoyment, but not in a daily newspapers. Carol Mitchell's suggestion that material like Page Three is harmful for young boys echoes concerns expressed by women in the oldest cohort. (Conversely, none expressed concerns about the effects such material might have on the sexuality of a growing girl). A moralistic vocabulary also featured in two hostile accounts given by the youngest cohort. Sharon Owens (aged 18 G3) said that Page Three was not 'very nice' and was 'wrong', whilst another suggested that the widespread availability of Page Three was a problem.

> I don't think - it's not very nice to look at other people's bodies all the time.
>
> Mandy Mitchell, aged 17 (G3)

A feminist vocabulary was an important way of talking about Page Three within the hostile accounts of all three cohorts. However, as shown below, there were differences in the content of the vocabulary according to whether it was used by the oldest or the middle and youngest cohorts. There were six examples of a feminist vocabulary in the hostile accounts given by the oldest cohort. Two women interpreted Page Three as having detrimental consequences for women's status, with Rene Evans (aged 82, G1) saying that it was 'cheapening' and Agnes Baker (aged 78, G1) saying that it was 'a skit on women'. Three women said that Page Three might be linked to sexual violence, because men might become 'disturbed' by the images of women it conveyed. For example:

> I think it makes men - it may disturb them when they see that...
>
> Alice Nicholl, aged 78 (G1)

> I do think it has an effect on men, I do really. A bad effect really. I think that's why there is so many rapes and assaults today.
>
> Yvonne Daniels, aged 75 (G1)

This concern emerged as a frequent theme in the letters received by Clare Short (Tunks and Hutchinson 1991) and in the survey conducted by *Woman* magazine cited earlier. However, no women of the other cohorts argued that material such as Page Three is a cause of sexual violence.

Only one woman of the oldest cohort directly used the feminist concept of objectification. Doris Ascote (aged 72, G1) said that Page Three encouraged men to think of women as 'just objects for their entertainment'. This explicitly feminist vocabulary was more apparent in the hostile accounts of the two younger cohorts. Seven examples of a feminist vocabulary were identified in each of the middle and youngest cohorts' hostile accounts. In these accounts, Page Three was described as having deleterious effects on women's status. For example:

> It's denigrating, isn't it.
>
> Angharad Baker, aged 50 (G2)

> ...I think it does cheapen women.
>
> Shirley Owens, aged 45 (G2)

> ...its degrading for women...to do that.
>
> Ruth Richards, aged 17 (G3)

Two women of the middle cohort and three women of the youngest cohort used the term 'sex object', as part of their description of the negative effects Page Three has on women's status. For example:

> It does encourage men to think of women purely as sex objects.
>
> Cynthia Daniels, aged 53 (G2)

> [It] just reinforces [women], really, as sex objects.
>
> Hayley Baker, aged 23 (G3)

> They [are] looked upon as objects for sex and not as themselves.
>
> Rebecca Daniels, aged 29 (G3)

> They do see them as sex objects...//...They should just see them as a normal person.
>
> Kirsty Harvey, aged 19 (G3)

In the above quotations, the women expand upon the phrase 'sex objects', interpreting Page Three as distorting the individuality of women, or at least, the individuality of Page Three models as women. In another example, the widespread effects of the objectification of the sexuality of individual Page Three models are clearly emphasised through use of the collective 'we':

> It makes the women look, well, as if they are dumb. If that's all we got to offer, as if they got no sense.
>
> Lorraine Morgan, aged 19 (G3)

One woman of the youngest cohort gave a particularly hostile account of Page Three, describing it as 'pornographic'. She went on to describe the effect Page Three has on men:

> ...I think if it doesn't directly effect their own lives, it effects something subtly in them that must sort of influence the things they do and the way they sort of see things.
>
> Hayley Baker, aged 23 (G3)

The consequences of Page Three on men was thus portrayed as subtle and pervasive.

A vocabulary of individualism was also present within hostile accounts of Page Three. Here, clear statements of disapproval were accompanied by a caveat which recognised that Page Three was an outcome of choices made by the models who appeared on it. Two women of the youngest cohort and one each in the older cohorts employed this vocabulary within their hostile accounts. For example:

> If they want to show their bodies, it's up to them.
>
> Yvonne Daniels, aged 75 (G1)

> If those girls want to do it, it's entirely up to them...
>
> Judith Ascote, aged 48 (G2)

> You can get money in other ways, not [by] showing themselves. But again, it is up to them if they want to do it.
>
> Ruth Richards, aged 17 (G3)

Hostile accounts of Page Three thus constructed it as material which had negative effects, either in moral terms or in terms of being detrimental to women's status in society. However, the right to pose nude for Page Three was recognised by some women.

'Sympathetic' accounts

Twenty eight accounts were categorised as being 'sympathetic' toward Page Three, with women of the younger cohorts giving more sympathetic accounts (10 and 11) than the older cohort (7). Across the three cohorts, a vocabulary of little consequence was the most prominent way of talking about Page Three. One feature of this vocabulary set was the claim that Page Three was not a problematical or a relevant issue for the women themselves:

> Doesn't bother me one way or the other...if my husband wishes to look at it, then it doesn't make any difference. (laughs)
>
> Nancy Caswell, aged 69 (G1)

Similarly, Janice Caswell (aged 44, G2) said that she did not give Page Three 'a lot of thought', whilst Gwen Keating (aged 53, G2) reported that 'it doesn't worry me'. Women of the youngest cohort also denied Page Three was an issue of personal relevance:

> It's all right, doesn't worry me one way or the other.
>
> Bethan Parry, aged 24 (G3)

> It doesn't bother me. It's okay.
>
> Denise Nicholl, aged 27 (G3)

In each cohort, women said that they had no objections to their husbands, sons or boyfriends looking at Page Three. Some reported discussing the relative merits of a particular model with their husband or boyfriend:

> Like, he always asks my opinion, you know, "what do you think of her?", like.
>
> Elaine Griffiths, aged 19 (G3)

Furthermore two women of the middle cohort reported their own admiration for Page Three models:

> I look at them and admire. If I see a Page Three girl and I just think, oh yes, she is lovely, she is lovely, or not.
>
> Angela Farrall, aged 44 (G2)

> *[Do you know what Page Three is?]*
> Yes. It is gorgeous women that I would like to look like.
>
> Vera Nicholl, aged 56 (G2)

A further feature of the vocabulary which posited Page Three as a matter of little consequence were references to other examples of public nudity in society:

> ...you go abroad now and even in this country on some beaches, you see the women topless, don't you? And I don't think the men take any notice of that.
>
> Nancy Caswell, aged 69 (G1)

> There has always been strip clubs...
>
> Angela Farrall, aged 44 (G2)

> I mean, I walked round topless [on holiday]. And it doesn't matter really...But Page Three, really, like I said, so many people go topless and things, it's nothing today.
>
> Wendy Caswell, aged 22 (G3)

In particular, the example of women going topless on beaches was given to suggest that Page Three is unremarkable. In the words of Rose Jessop (aged 73, G1) "its nothing, today, is it?" Other women drew a parallel with being naked in the bath with their young children in order to account for their not minding if their children saw a Page Three picture. One drew a distinction between the Page Three feature and pictures of partially clothed women in other tabloid newspapers:

> It don't bother me to look at [Page Three]. What I don't like is the [*Sunday*] *Sport*, that one. Because, I mean, it's on every bloody page...
>
> Donna Powell, aged 24 (G3)

Here, the principle of Page Three (as a picture of partially clothed women in provocative sexual poses) is not at issue but the rather the *proliferation* of such pictures.

Women giving sympathetic accounts of Page Three tended to deny that there were any negative consequences in terms of how men regard women, that it was merely 'harmless fun':

> Oh, it's nothing. It's just a bit of fun for the men to look at (laughs).
>
> Sarah Mitchell, aged 64 (G1)

> [Its] totally harmless. I mean, we like looking at lovely men, don't we?
>
> Vera Nicholl, aged 56 (G2)

> I don't think it's harmful really. It's just a bit of fun, really.
>
> Rhian Keating, aged 24 (G3)

Some women of the middle cohort described Page Three as having positive outcomes, particularly for the models themselves. For example,

> [They] get paid damn good money for it. I mean, really and truly, the women have the last laugh, don't they?...So all the men that go "oohher" and all this, she is laughing all the way to the bank...
>
> Janice Caswell, aged 44 (G2)

> They are making a living out of it. They are exploiting their public.
>
> Maureen Richards, aged 38 (G2)

A vocabulary of individualism was also an important way in which accounts sympathetic toward Page Three were expressed, particularly for women of the middle and youngest cohort. Here, reference was made to it being 'up to' the individual models who appear as Page Three 'girls', or to the person who gains pleasure from looking at Page Three:

> *[Do you disapprove of Page Three?]*
> It doesn't bother me. No, if they want to do it, that's their trade.
>
> Doreen Owens, aged 70 (G1)

> If they want to sit there flaunting themselves, it's entirely up to them.
>
> Janice Caswell, aged 44 (G2)

> If that's what someone wants to look at.
>
> Rita Parry, aged 42 (G2)

> I mean, the girl who's had her picture taken has put herself up for it. It's up to her.
>
> Eryl Thomas, aged 17 (G3)

In sympathetic accounts, Page Three was constructed as a matter of little consequence, especially in the light of nudity elsewhere in contemporary society. Rather than negative effects being recognised, Page Three was said to have beneficial outcomes, both as a form of harmless entertainment for men and in financial terms for Page Three models themselves. Moreover, in sympathetic accounts, emphasis was laid on the right of the individual Page Three model to choose to appear in such a publication and to display her body in that manner.

Conclusions

This chapter has reported on accounts of Page Three, a publication which represents women's sexuality for men's consumption. Analysis of data generated by interview questions has shown that cohort influenced women's responses to Page Three and the language they used to convey these responses. Women in the oldest cohort tended to give hostile accounts of Page Three and used vocabularies which constructed it as an affront to morality and an affront to the status of women. In contrast, women in the younger cohorts tended to give accounts which were sympathetic toward Page Three. They used vocabularies which constructed Page Three as an issue of little consequence and also suggested that the decision to appear partially nude was 'up to' the models themselves.

The women's responses to Page Three were comprised of four distinctive vocabulary sets, present in the accounts of all three cohorts. A morality vocabulary, found in hostile accounts, described Page Three as 'not nice' and as 'disgusting'. The depiction of partially clothed women in daily newspapers was suggested to be inappropriate and to encourage interest in sex, particularly amongst young boys. In this vocabulary set, which was especially made use of by the oldest cohort, Page Three was interpreted as a publication with negative effects. However, it was boys and men about whom concern was expressed rather than girls or women. In the morality vocabulary, therefore, Page Three was constructed as a gender issue, but in terms of boys' and men's interest in sex rather than the objectification of women's bodies and the effects this has on women's status and position in society.

Hostile accounts were also comprised of a feminist vocabulary. This way of talking about Page Three featured in the accounts of all three cohorts and, unlike on other issues, was not especially associated with younger cohorts. Within the feminist vocabulary, Page Three was constructed as a publication which represented women in a degrading manner, via its depiction of women as 'sex objects'. Links were made between the objectification of individual Page Three models and the effects on women as a collective grouping. Some in the oldest cohort suggested that Page Three-type publications had negative effects on women in more direct ways, through causing rapes and sexual assaults. Within the feminist vocabulary, Page Three was constructed as a highly significant gender issue, via its detrimental effects on women's status, and personal safety. Although this vocabulary set was employed by each cohort to a comparable extent, there were notable differences between the cohorts in its explicitness. In particular, the younger cohorts more frequently used the term 'sex objects' when describing the impact Page Three has on women.

Accounts sympathetic toward Page Three were comprised mainly of a vocabulary which posited the publication as being of minimal personal relevance[1] (see also Pursehouse 1991) or of little social consequence. Here Page Three was said to be just one example of the acceptability of nudity in contemporary society. For example, women referred to public nudity on beaches and private nudity in front of young children. In citing such examples, the distinction between Page Three as a *representation* of women in sexually provocative poses, produced for men's pleasure and enjoyment, and 'natural' nudity was unrecognised. Page Three was argued to have no negative effects, but instead was regarded as a source of 'harmless' fun for men. Some women using this vocabulary set also reported discussing the merits of Page Three models with their male partners, or claimed to be unconcerned if their husbands or sons looked at it. Others said that they were envious of the beauty and physical attributes of Page Three models. Within this vocabulary set, therefore, Page Three was not constructed as a gender issue, at least not in the sense that it was seen to have detrimental effects on gender relations. A vocabulary of individualism was also used within sympathetic accounts and was especially made use of by women in the younger cohorts. This vocabulary contained suggestions that Page Three models had the right to choose whether or not to pose semi-nude and also that readers of Page Three and its host newspaper had the right to look at it if they wanted to. In employing a vocabulary of individualism, especially where reference was made to the freedom of choice of models to appear on Page Three, the women denied the consequences of such choices for women as a whole and for how they are represented in society. This position is directly against the feminist hostile vocabulary on Page Three, which maintained that individual Page Three models represent a denigration and objectification of women as a collectivity (see also Rowland 1984).

The contrasting responses to Page Three according to cohort and the differences in vocabularies employed when discussing the issue are in keeping with what is known about the women's different 'locations' in historical time. As noted in Chapter Five, historical evidence, and the women's own accounts, suggest that sexuality in the past was largely a private matter and not open for public discussion or consumption through cultural representations. The socialisation experiences of the oldest cohort in relation to sex and nudity is reflected in their greater hostility toward Page Three and in their more frequent use of a moralistic vocabulary, compared to younger cohorts. These women's location in historical time, via their life course and cohort membership, also explains why they made more limited use of the individualist vocabulary. However, women of this cohort also used a feminist vocabulary, constructing Page Three as a publication which degraded women (the significance of this finding is discussed below).

The responses of the middle and youngest cohorts, and the vocabularies they used, also suggests an interpretation in terms of their location in historical time. Given the widespread availability of sexually explicit materials since the 1960s and the more liberal sexual moral climate, Page Three was mostly regarded as a harmless and tame publication. Women of the younger cohorts therefore tended to construct Page Three as an issue of little consequence. These women's location in historical time was also reflected in their greater use of a vocabulary of individualism, particularly by the youngest cohort. As argued in previous chapters, the claiming of individuals' rights to self-determination and free choice has become an increasingly acceptable 'vocabulary of motive' in the post-war decades. The hostile accounts of women in the younger cohorts, moreover, were mostly constructed with a feminist vocabulary and more explicitly so than where used by the oldest cohort. It is a plausible argument that the feminist vocabulary was a more appropriate and acceptable vocabulary than 'morality' to employ in hostile accounts given by the younger cohorts. Their location in historical time means that they have had greater exposure to second wave feminism which, via campaigns against beauty contests (for example) has had representations of women and the objectification of their bodies as central concerns.

In comparison with findings on other gender issues reported in this study, cohort differences in accounts of Page Three and in vocabularies used to discuss it, are notably distinctive. Analyses undertaken in previous chapters has shown that it was the oldest cohort who were invariably the most traditional in their construction of gender issues and the younger cohorts who were the more progressive and feminist-leaning. However, on the issue of Page Three, it was the oldest cohort who, in giving predominantly hostile accounts, problematised it in a manner congruent with feminist analyses. In part, this finding is a reflection of the 'uncomfortable alliance' between the anti-pornography positions taken by moralists and by some feminists. The target of their respective critiques is the same, although the grounds on which their critiques are based differ substantially. Indeed, an important vocabulary for conveying hostility to Page Three for the oldest cohort was moral in content. Such a vocabulary was much less evident in the hostile accounts of the younger cohorts. However, and in contrast with other gender issues, the women of the oldest cohort did also employ a feminist hostile vocabulary (albeit in a less explicit form than that used by younger women). Arguably, the comparatively greater use of a feminist vocabulary on Page Three by the oldest cohort was a consequence of the degree of congruence between moral and (some) feminist critiques of pornography. In other words, the similarity of the critiques (or at least their shared target) may have provided an airing for feminist discourse, thereby making it more available and/or acceptable to older women on this issue than for other gender issues.

The finding that it was the younger cohort rather than the oldest who, in being predominantly sympathetic towards Page Three, were out of step with feminist critiques is in marked contrast to cohort patterns that emerged elsewhere in this study. On issues of gender roles, equality, abortion and sexual preference, it was the younger cohorts who made use of vocabularies in keeping with progressive, feminist constructions of these issues, but this was not the case for Page Three. However, as indicated by the *British Social Attitudes* survey discussed earlier, other data on age differences in attitudes toward pornography also show that it is younger women who are more tolerant of sexually explicit material than older women. These findings confirm that pornography is a problematic issue for feminism. Calls made by some feminists for the prohibition or tighter regulation of pornography arguably contradict with liberal-individualist values of freedom of choice and of expression (this is a tension reflected in the existence of feminist groupings which campaign against censorship of pornography - see Assiter and Carol 1993; Rodgerson and Wilson 1991, for example). Furthermore, in opposing pornography, some feminists find themselves on the same side as moralists. By association, these feminists may be tainted with criticism that they too are illiberal, puritanical, anti-sex prudes. For these reasons, amongst the middle and youngest cohorts, feminist discourses on pornography may have been overridden by libertarian, individualist discourses informed by sexual liberalism.

Compared to explicit hard-core pornography, Page Three and other examples of the pornographic genre are tame and the women's responses to it may not be representative of their responses to the range of other media which objectify women's bodies for men's enjoyment. Nevertheless, the findings reported in this chapter indicate that the issue of the cultural representation of women's bodies is a highly problematic one for feminism, and more so than any other issue examined in the study. The relationship between feminism and its main constituency, women, is explored further in the next chapter through an examination of responses to the organised women's movement and its activists.

Notes

1. In the interviews with the women, questions on Page Three immediately followed, in most cases, a set of questions on homosexuality and lesbianism. In retrospect, I feel that the positioning of these questions, one after the other, was insensitive. It may have encouraged some of the women to employ a vocabulary of little consequence, in order that I did not think they were lesbian. Although I have no firm evidence to support this interpretation, I felt that some women regarded the Page Three questions as trick questions, whose real purpose was to establish their sexual

orientation. In later interviews, I endeavoured to keep the two questions apart to avoid this possibility.

7. 'Making things better for women' or 'going over the top'?: Accounts of feminism

The history of British feminism as a social and political movement in the past is reasonably well documented, and the vitality and range of contemporary feminist discourse is indicated by a significant body of academic writing. In these various ways, we have evidence on what British feminism has been in the past and is currently. Yet, there is little evidence on *responses* to feminism as a social and political movement, of how it is interpreted and understood in the everyday world. Feminism aims to change how women are perceived, but surprisingly little is known about how the messages it sends out are perceived, especially by women themselves. In debates about the nature and significance of feminism, the understandings and conceptions women hold about feminism have, then, been rather neglected.

Given that the considerable changes in gender relations in the twentieth century have at least partly been brought about by feminism, the lack of evidence on women's responses to the organised women's movement is quite remarkable. The rather hybrid collection of available data is really only suggestive of the standing feminism has amongst its main constituency, women. It is known that feminism and feminists have long faced hostility from certain quarters of society. In Britain, for example, Mary Wollstonecraft was described as a 'hyena in petticoats' in 1792 (Neustatter 1990), whilst the suffragists were depicted as ugly, mannish spinsters by the Edwardian press. Activists of the 'second wave' of the women's movement in the 1970s were similarly depicted as 'unattractive man-haters' (Holdsworth 1988: 185-6, 198). The practice of equating feminism with lesbianism has been used since the turn of the century in order to scare women away from feminism, and to dismiss and compartmentalise women who are feminists (Tuttle 1986; see also Rowland 1984). Furthermore, the abbreviations 'women's lib.' and 'women's libbers', and the term 'bra burners'[1] have been interpreted as 'demeaning' and as 'trivialising' the women's movement and its activists (Tuttle 1986: 361). In contemporary Britain, the phrase "I'm not a feminist but..." is widely recognised as a standard way for women to distance themselves from feminism, whilst simultaneously agreeing with aspects of its agenda. The apparent negativity with which feminism is perceived in contemporary Britain is further indicated by newspaper surveys. For example, in 1991 *The Guardian* found that most respondents believed feminism was frowned upon (*The Guardian*, March 7th 1991).

Social scientific evidence on British women's responses to feminism is lacking[2]. As Morgan and Wilcox (1992: 152) have noted, research has tended to focus on 'elite' feminist organisations rather than on 'mass attitudes' towards the feminist movement (for example, Rowland 1984; Wandor 1990). Some small-scale British studies have been undertaken. Oakley (1974) found that her sample of housewives held predominantly negative attitudes toward the women's liberation movement, whilst Griffin (1989) found that young women displayed attitudes that could be recognised as feminist, yet tended to avoid identifying themselves *as* feminists. Previous chapters have reported survey evidence which indicates age differences on what might be termed 'feminist attitudes' (for example, attitudes to gender roles, abortion and pornography). These data show that younger women hold more 'feminist' attitudes than older women. As in the present study, these findings were interpreted as functions of cohort, that is, as a consequence of their differing social and historical experiences, including their exposure to feminist arguments and the improved opportunities faced by women, especially in relation to paid work (Martin and Roberts 1984; Witherspoon 1985; Airey and Brook 1986). Although suggesting that younger women hold more 'feminist attitudes' than older women, it is not clear from the available data whether older and younger women share common responses to feminism as a social and political movement. The issue of age differences in women's understandings of and responses to feminism is an interesting one. As Schneider (1988) notes, the women's movement has always had aims of changing the way women are viewed, both by themselves and by men. Thus, she proposes, an examination of the ways women of different ages, given their differing social and historical experiences, view their lives and feminism is an important exercise. It raises questions about social and political change and notions of collective consciousness. Moreover, as others have noted (e.g. Renzetti 1987), the future growth and prosperity of feminism depends greatly on its attractiveness to new members, who will develop and sustain it in years to come. If contemporary young women are found to respond negatively to feminism, questions are therefore raised about its future. Given the gaps in knowledge about women's responses to feminism, not least how these may vary by age, asking women in this study for their conceptions of feminism and feminists was a key concern. Before reporting the findings, it is first necessary to sketch a broad history of feminism during the life time of the women whose accounts are the focus of this study, particularly in terms of its changing profile and fortunes.

Feminism in Britain in the twentieth century

The historical development of feminism in Britain can be divided into five more or less distinct phases. First, the nineteenth century, when the central concern was 'equality' including in employment, legal rights over property and custody of children and the right to vote. In the second phase, during the early decades of the twentieth century, the struggle for the vote emerged as the predominant concern. Accordingly, feminists of this early period have been characterised as using the vocabulary of 'rights' and 'equality' (Banks 1981). The struggle for suffrage bestowed unity on 'the women's movement' (as it was then called, see Alberti 1989; Dyhouse 1989), a unity which dissipated in the years after the vote had been achieved. This third period, of the inter-war years, was characterised by ideological and institutional divisions within the movement, which increasingly came to be referred to as 'feminism' (Banks 1981; Kent 1988; Alberti 1989). The 'new feminists' (a contemporary term) concentrated on issues such as family allowances or endowment, birth control and protective legislation. Priorities such as these were an anathema to egalitarian or equal rights feminists, whose fundamental emphasis was a reorientation of women away from the domestic sphere (Alberti 1989).

According to the title of Dale Spender's book (1982), there has always been a women's movement this century, yet activity seems to have been in abeyance following the divergence of the two feminisms in the 1920s and 1930s. The abeyance continued up until the 1970s (the 'second wave' of feminism). The 'ideological catalysts' (Randall 1982) of this fourth phase of the women's movement were undoubtedly the American liberation movements (that is, the black liberation movement, the student protest movement and the women's movement). Moreover, there was a vibrant culture of left-wing politics in Britain, as evidenced by the British student movements and the increased militancy of working class women. One example here is the 1968 Ford strike, where women workers demanded equal pay (Banks 1981). The late 1960s also saw the rise of women's groups and in 1970, the first national conference of the Women's Liberation Movement was held at Ruskin College, Oxford. The conference, amongst other things, defined the most immediate problems facing women as an oppressed group and four demands were formulated. The demands, which were to become the focus for demonstrating and campaigning, were: equal pay, equal education, twenty four hour nurseries, and free contraception and abortion (Wandor 1972). Other notable aspects of the 'second wave' movement were: the campaign against the 1970 Miss World contest, which encouraged the 'bra burning' myth; marches in London and Liverpool, with the four demands prominently displayed on banners; the addition of three further demands: an end to discrimination against lesbians and the right of all women to define their own sexuality; freedom from violence and sexual coercion; an end to all the laws, assumptions and institutions that perpetuate male dominance and men's aggression towards women (Segal 1987). Although the vocabulary of this period was primarily one of 'liberation', 'oppression' and of women uniting together as a 'sisterhood' (Randall 1982), there was continuity with earlier phases via concerns over 'equal rights'. The 'second wave' also saw the setting up of national organisations such as the Women's Aid Federation, the National Abortion Campaign, Rape Crisis Centres (Coote and Campbell 1987) and the rise of the women's peace movement centred around the Greenham Common nuclear missile base in Berkshire (Neustatter 1990). As shown below, many of the activities and achievements of the 'second wave' of feminism featured in the women's accounts. It is important to note, though, that during the 1960s and 1970s, women organising together was not called 'feminism'. This was a position adopted by or ascribed to particular groups, for example, the radical or revolutionary feminists within the Women's Liberation Movement (Delmar 1986).

The fifth historical phase of feminism had parallels with the third phase, in that following a period of strength, unity and a high public profile, the movement became characterised by divisions: this time between the radical or revolutionary feminists and others of more 'liberal' views. Writing in 1987, Segal notes that it has been 'many years since we could talk meaningfully of any single entity called "the women's movement"' and points to the last national conference in 1978 and the decline of locally based networks that were a characteristic feature of the movement at its height. There has been some funding for women's groups of various kinds from local councils, but these are isolated and do not form part of a national or regional network (Segal 1987: 56-57). Since the fragmentation of the Women's Liberation Movement, there has been a gradual replacement of the term 'women's liberation' by the term 'feminism'. This change in vocabulary is argued to represent a move from a position of common revolutionary struggle to a more restricted, realistic and less revolutionary orientation (Wier and Wilson 1984: 79).

Although no longer an active, campaigning political movement with a high public profile, feminism survives as a body of thought with powerful social influence and considerable ideological impact. Segal (1987) argues that feminism is popular and commercially successful, as evidenced by the fact that its ideas appear in many popular magazines. In academia, the body of empirical, theoretical and philosophical work, across a range of disciplines, is further testimony to the continuing importance and influence of feminism, despite 'post-feminism' and the anti-feminist 'backlash' (Faludi 1992; Walby 1993).

Accounts of feminism

Data on the women's responses to feminism are mainly drawn from their replies to a series of questions, which were posed toward the end of the interviews. If, by this time, it had not already come up, I introduced the issue of feminism by asking the women if they knew what 'feminism' (and/or 'women's liberation') was. Further questions aimed to produce descriptions of the aims and concerns of 'feminism' (or 'women's liberation') and identifications of individuals who were believed to be 'feminists' (or 'women's liberationists'). The women were also asked whether they thought of themselves as a 'feminist' (or 'women's liberationist'). On the basis of replies to this series of questions, and associated probe questions, each women's account was categorised either as mainly 'hostile' or mainly 'sympathetic' in content. Table Six illustrates the distribution of hostile and sympathetic accounts by cohort.

Table 6   Accounts of Feminism

	Oldest Cohort	Middle Cohort	Youngest Cohort	TOTAL
'Mainly Hostile'	8	2	3	13
'Mainly Sympathetic'	8	16	16	40
'Don't know'	3	1	-	4
TOTAL	19	19	19	57

A clear majority of the sample gave accounts which were categorised as mainly sympathetic towards feminism. However, the data show marked differences between the oldest cohort and the younger cohorts. The oldest cohort appeared more equivocal in their responses, with equal numbers giving mainly hostile or mainly sympathetic accounts. Moreover, three of these women reported that they did not know what either 'feminism' or 'women's liberation' was. In contrast, very few women in the younger cohorts gave mainly hostile accounts and only one reported that she was unfamiliar with both 'feminism' and 'women's liberation'. This finding is one indication of the several ways familiarity with feminism differed according to cohort (see below). Another was the way in which the younger cohorts frequently introduced the issue *themselves* at an earlier point in the interview than I would have generally raised it. Around a third (seven out of nineteen in each case, including four mother-daughter pairs) of the younger cohorts independently introduced the issue compared to no women of the oldest cohort.

The lack of familiarity with the terms 'feminism' and 'feminists' was especially evident amongst the oldest cohort. Only one (out of 19) said she had heard of feminism, describing it as 'raising the conditions for women', especially via 'equal pay for equal work' (Rene Evans, aged 82, G1). Eleven other women of this cohort also said they had heard of 'feminism', but they misinterpreted it to mean 'feminine qualities', either in women or in men. For example:

[Do you know what feminism is?]
I can say to you, "that person there is very feminine, isn't she?", but I don't really know what feminism means...I know what it means to me by looking at somebody. I can't pinpoint it really, no.

Lillian Thomas, aged 75 (G1)

(pause) Well, I think it is to do with a woman and her make up, her perfumes and different things like that. That's what I would say it is.

Nora Lestor, aged 72 (G1)

Feminism? Well, the only thing I can think of is like a man acting like a woman. Is that what you mean?

Yvonne Daniels, aged 75 (G1)

Women of this cohort were much more familiar with the term 'women's liberation' and its abbreviation, 'women's lib.' (only three did not know what it was) and were able to offer 'appropriate' descriptions of its aims and concerns. In seven cases, 'equality' was identified as a central concern, either through direct use of the term or indirectly, through references to 'having a say' or 'being a bus driver'. Women of this cohort also made references to 'freedom', to independence and to women 'being their own bosses'. In identifying the aims and concerns of 'women's liberation', the oldest-cohort used vaguer terms and appeared hesitant and unsure, compared to the younger cohorts (see below).

Only three out of nineteen women of the middle cohort reported that they had not heard of 'feminism' or could not say what it was (one of the three also reported not knowing what women's liberation was either). However, four women misinterpreted 'feminism' to mean femininity. For example:

> Feminism, yeah.// Well, I suppose - I don't know really. Well, you say, very feminine. I suppose it is someone who doesn't like to get their hands dirty, you know...And always doing their hair and doing their eyelashes.
>
> Carol Mitchell, aged 38 (G2)

However, unlike the oldest cohort, none interpreted 'feminism' to mean effeminacy or any quality found in men. All but one of the middle cohort reported knowing what either feminism and/or women's liberation was and were able to offer 'appropriate' descriptions of its aims and concerns. The women's movement was almost exclusively described in terms of equality of rights (17 cases).

Of the three cohorts, the youngest were the most familiar with the term 'feminism'. Sixteen out of nineteen women indicated that they knew what feminism was, and moreover, were able to offer an appropriate description of it. Only three women reported that they had not heard of feminism or that they did not know what it was. All were able to offer a description of women's liberation. Like their mothers, women of the youngest cohort mostly spoke of the women's movement as being concerned with equality of rights (17 cases). However, the greater familiarity of the youngest cohort with the women's movement was further reflected in their tendency to attribute a wider range of aims and concerns to it. These included references to freedom, assertiveness, independence and the sexual objectification of women, via such examples as opposition to 'Page Three' and opposition to wearing make-up, shaving legs and armpits, and wearing bras.

Another feature of the accounts of the youngest cohort was the distinctions they made between different types or degrees of feminism, including 'militant feminists', 'hard feminists', 'very radical feminists', 'strong feminists', 'left-wing feminists' and 'ultra ultra feminists'. Such distinctions were employed in explanations detailing responses to the women's movement, including in definitions of persons who were thought to be feminists and in their own self-identification as feminists. For example:

[Do you think of yourself as a feminist?]
No. Well, people say I am.//...I suppose I am but not hard (laughs).// Well, I'm not really really "women this, women that". I just think they should do what they want without being stopped by people from doing it.

Ruth Richards, aged 17 (G3)

These distinctions between types or degrees of feminism drawn by the youngest cohort were not found in the accounts of the older cohorts. This is a further indication of the greater familiarity of the youngest cohort with feminism, including with the existence of different versions of feminism and, arguably, with the extent to which 'feminist' is a problematical identity. In employing these distinctions, the youngest cohort were marginalising 'extreme' feminism through language. Yet, this practice allowed them to report a sympathy for and an identification with a 'weaker' version of 'mainstream' feminism. Indeed, eleven women of the youngest cohort defined themselves as feminists in one way or another, compared to seven women of the middle cohort and only two women of the oldest cohort.

Hostile vocabularies

Analysis of the women's accounts of feminism led to the identification of two hostile vocabularies. The first, *feminism as extremism*, was comprised of general references to feminism 'going too far' or 'being over the top', as well as descriptions of ways in which this extremism manifests itself. Thus feminism was said to use unnecessary or inappropriate tactics or methods which alienated the public and reduced support for the aims of the women's movement. Feminism was also said to be extreme in being 'against men' and as being 'sexist' towards them. Women identified as feminists were individuals with negative personality traits, such as obsessiveness, selfishness and a domineering manner. The second hostile vocabulary posited feminism and its adherents as *contrary to femininity*. Feminism was said to threaten certain valued feminine privileges, including courtesy shown to women by men and 'being treated like a woman'. Furthermore, individuals identified as feminists were described as lacking in femininity, including in terms of being lesbian in sexual orientation.

General references to feminism as extremism were found in the accounts of all three cohorts to the same extent (four examples each). Here, feminism was directly said to be 'extreme', or, in the words of Dorothy Powell (aged 79, G1) to 'go too far with things, really'. The implication within this vocabulary is that whilst on the whole the aims of feminism are laudable ones, either the extent of the changes sought or the methods used are 'a bit too much' (Doris Ascote, aged 72, G1):

> I agree with some of it, but they go over the top.
> Elaine Griffiths, aged 19 (G3)

Some women identified particular approaches or particular tactics as 'going over the top' which had the effect of 'getting people's backs up' (Rita Parry, aged 42, G2):

> I didn't agree with...Greenpeace [*sic - Greenham*], ...I didn't like, back a few years ago, with women sitting around outside the gates and things like that. I didn't think that was right.
> Shirley Owens, aged 45 (G2)

> ...I suppose there's bound to be some good in it but some of it is silly I think.// You know, years ago there was burning your bra and all that marching and all that. I don't believe in all that (....). I don't think that gets anybody anywhere.
> Carol Mitchell, aged 38 (G2)

These women agreed with the broad aims of the women's movement but were disapproving of methods or strategies it followed. A further theme within the feminism as extremism vocabulary interpreted feminism as being 'against men', a target which was regarded as unfair and inappropriate:

> Oh, I don't agree with women's lib.// No.// Well, I think they go over the top with it.// Well, I think they go too far...they try to make men inferior...
> Vera Nicholl, aged 56 (G2)

In another example of this vocabulary, Mrs Thatcher was not thought to be a 'woman's libber' since she was 'fair to both men and women' (Alice Nicholl, aged 78, G1). The implication here is that women's liberationists are not fair to men. The construction of feminism as being 'against men' was especially prominent in the accounts of the youngest cohort (5 examples, compared to 3 identified in the oldest and 1 identified in the middle cohort's accounts):

> Well, I think feminists are anti-men. I mean, that's the way it comes over to me. Just anti-men.
>
> Karen Lestor, aged 29 (G3)

In other examples, feminists were said to take things 'too far' by being 'sexist' (Elaine Griffiths, aged 19, G3) and were described as being 'on the same par as chauvinists, as male chauvinists' (Lindsay Farrall, aged 20, G3).

Another aspect of the vocabulary of extremism was the attribution of negative personality traits, either to individual women who were thought to be feminists or in terms of a general tendency in such women. This way of conveying hostility to the women's movement was especially prominent within the accounts of the oldest cohort (6 examples), compared to its presence within the accounts of the middle (3 examples) and youngest (2 examples) cohorts. Individuals identified as feminists were characterised as obsessive and manic in their beliefs and opinions:

> ...some of them are on about it all the time. That's their life isn't it...somebody Greer...I can't stand her for the simple reason that is all she can talk about.
>
> Sarah Mitchell, aged 64 (G1)

> *[Why did you say 'ranting'?]*
> That's the other thing, you see, you think of. Well, if you're thinking in your mind, "what's a feminist". Sort of "bloody men, don't do anything".
>
> Eryl Thomas, aged 17 (G3)

Denise Nicholl (aged 27, G3) identified a female relative who corresponded to her conception of a feminist, primarily because she was 'always lecturing' to Denise, telling her 'don't do this, don't do that'. In characterisations of women thought to be feminists, references were also made to other unflattering, extreme personality traits, including selfishness and a domineering manner:

> Well, they [women's liberationists] are usually all sort of for themselves, I think...
>
> Carol Mitchell, aged 38 (G2)

> *[What would it be about a woman that would make you think she was a feminist?]*
> Just her attitude, I think, a domineering attitude. I think a lot of social workers...they seem to fit into a mould.
>
> Rita Parry, aged 42 (G2)

Using Mrs Thatcher as a probe produced the following characterisation of women's liberationists:

> Well, she could be anything. I tell you what she is - a dictator. If that's women's lib. - yes.
>
> Sybil Richards, aged 71 (G1)

> Yes, in lots of ways.// She thinks she knows it all. And nobody else knows anything, only her. She has got that idea. She is the only one who is right.
>
> Doris Ascote, aged 72 (G1)

These examples interpret Mrs Thatcher's perceived characteristic of dominance as being akin to personality traits of a women's liberationist. The attribution of such personality characteristics was a feature of the hostile vocabularies of women's liberation aside from Mrs Thatcher[3]. For example:

> *[Do you know anyone who you think of as a woman's libber, in your family, or friends?]*
> One of my friends, she's a very dominant personality and it doesn't matter what you do, she's the boss and nothing will alter her.
>
> Edith Parry, aged 75 (G1)

The second vocabulary set which conveyed hostility toward the women's movement constructed feminism as contrary to femininity. Two women of the oldest cohort suggested that identifying with the aims and objectives of feminism directly contradicted 'being treated like a woman'. For example:

> *[Do you think of yourself as a woman's libber?]*
> (laughs) I doubt it very much. All I am is a woman. You know. I like what women do and I like to be treated like a woman.
>
> Doreen Owens, aged 70 (G1)

Similarly, according to two women in the middle cohort, identification with the women's movement on a personal level conflicted with their liking for the 'privileges of femininity' and courtesies shown by men to women, including opening doors and giving flowers:

> ...I mean, I think it's nice, if you go on a bus that a man will stand up for you... And I mean, I don't want to be a man and I would like to be treated like a woman. *[So you are not a women's libber then?]* Oh, definitely not. No.
> Vera Nicholl, aged 56 (G2)

In these examples, being a feminist or a women's liberationist is associated with the loss of being 'treated like a woman'. Only one woman of the youngest cohort made reference to her liking for 'being treated like a woman' by men as a reason for not identifying with feminism but another did imply that there was an unavoidable contradiction between femininity and feminism:

> I don't think (laughing) you can be a woman and be anti-men.
> Karen Lestor, aged 29 (G3)

Within the vocabulary which posited feminism as contrary to femininity, hostile characterisations of women thought to be feminists were also made. The alleged lack of femininity of feminists was said to be evident in their behaviour, appearance and style of clothing and in their sexuality. Three examples were found in the accounts of the middle and youngest cohorts (six in total):

> *[Do you think Mrs Thatcher is a woman's libber?]*
> Oh she is definitely.// Well, she is getting more like a man everyday, so. (pause) I don't know. And I don't think they're that feminine, you know.
> Joan Lestor, aged 51 (G2)

> I think you always get the impression with women's libbers and women's righters, that they're big butch lesbians.
> Rita Parry, aged 42 (G2)

> Yeah, when you said it, I thought of somebody. I don't know why, somebody on Greenham Common, with - like a lesbian.
> Wendy Caswell, aged 22 (G3)

It was noted earlier in the chapter that associations between women's movement activists and a lack of femininity (including in terms of homosexuality) has a long history as a component of hostility toward the women's movement, and one that stretches back at least to the eighteenth century. In the women's accounts such associations formed part of a wider vocabulary of feminism as a threat to feminine privileges and a denial or rejection of femininity.

In summary, hostile vocabularies of the women's movement constructed it as immoderate and its adherents were identified as individuals with unpleasant personalities, especially by women of the oldest cohort. For women of the youngest cohort who used hostile vocabularies in their accounts, the extremism of feminism primarily manifested itself through being 'anti-men'. Otherwise, hostile vocabularies represented feminism as undermining valued aspects of femininity (primarily through outlawing courtesies shown by men to women), and feminists as lacking in femininity. This hostile vocabulary was particularly made use of by women of the middle and youngest cohorts.

Sympathetic vocabularies

Within the women's accounts, a vocabulary was identified which, in various ways, constructed *feminism as commendable.* Here, the aims of feminism were seen as valuable and proper and it was also said to have had success in achieving them. Concrete achievements of feminism were identified and were regarded as meritorious. Moreover, although feminism was regarded as a success, its work was said to be unfinished since much inequality between women and men remains in society. Individual women identified as feminists were admired and were attributed with positive, role model-like characteristics. A further element of this vocabulary set were statements of disapproval toward hostile depictions and stereotyping of feminists.

Women employing a feminism as commendable vocabulary interpreted the aims and achievements as valuable and appropriate ones. For example:

> *[What would you say that women's lib. was?]*
> Well that's having the rights of anything. Yes. I think we could do with a bit more of that.
>
> Rose Jessop, aged 73 (G1)

> *[Do you think it has achieved anything, women's liberation?]*
> Oh yes. Definitely.// ...now they have got more opportunities, haven't they? They are allowed to do work now, that they weren't allowed to do years ago. I think that is an achievement.
>
> Nancy Caswell, aged 69 (G1)

Such positive endorsements of the aims and achievements of feminism were more frequent and more strongly stated within the accounts of the younger cohorts. Achievements of the women's movement tended to be identified in a general sense:

> I think it has achieved a lot for different people, in different fields, in different ways.
>
> Janice Caswell, aged 44 (G2)

> I suppose it's bound to improve things. Because over the years, things have improved for women. I suppose you have got to look back and say, well women's lib. have [*sic*] helped. Obviously.
>
> Carol Mitchell, aged 38 (G2)

Specific achievements, attributed to the women's movement were also cited, including the vote, and organisations such as Women's Aid and Rape Crisis Centres, employment tribunals, and equal pay and opportunities:

> Oh yes...we got the vote. Oh, it's changed a lot.
>
> Rita Parry, aged 42 (G2)

> I suppose so, they have. To a certain extent. I mean, they have got tribunals now, haven't they? If a woman, is, you know, if she thinks she is not getting the same as a man.
>
> Susan Griffiths, aged 44 (G2)

> I think it's achieved a lot now. Men's attitudes towards women. There's a lot more women in jobs and everything. A woman Prime Minister, which wouldn't have happened years ago. I think it's brought about all that change.
>
> Eryl Thomas, aged 17 (G3)

Women of the middle and youngest cohorts employing a sympathetic vocabulary suggested that whilst the women's movement had achieved some important advances, it had not been completely successful and more needed to be done in order further to improve the position of women. For example:

> I don't think that they have accomplished what they hoped to have accomplished.// Well I think it has achieved something but not enough, not nearly enough.
> Pauline Evans, aged 39 (G2)

> Oh I think it has achieved some things, yes. I think for *some* women, it's still got a long way to go.
> Maureen Richards, aged 38 (G2)

> *[Do you think feminism has achieved anything?]*
> It has done a lot. It's not done enough. And I know there is talk now of a post-feminist age. That's rubbish...because there are still *huge* distances before we get to whatever we want, equality or whatever. Whatever the aims are, we haven't reached them yet.
> Isabel Ascote, aged 21 (G3)

Such accounts are clearly sympathetic to the women's movement, both in the sense of recognising its achievements and in that the concerns of feminism are portrayed as proper and valid ones.

Several accounts of the middle and youngest cohort's were sympathetic toward feminism in the sense that they distanced themselves from the hostile coverage that they perceived feminist activities had received, for example Greenham Common, a women only anti-nuclear peace camp:

> ...there were some very nasty bits of publicity about that in the *Sun* and the *Mirror*. Quite unnecessary, I thought.
> Judith Ascote, aged 48 (G2)

> It's made people say, "Oh, they are a load of lesbians, what are they on about?". And it makes me mad because, all right, even if they are a load of lesbians, they believe in what they are doing.
> Janice Caswell, aged 44 (G2)

Several women of the youngest cohort similarly distanced themselves from the hostile coverage that the women's movement had received, or from the hostile stereotyping of activists:

> ...A lot of men think, with the women's liberation movement, that they are all weird, that they are all lesbians working together.
>
> Lindsay Farrall, aged 20 (G3)

> *[What is it about a person that makes you think they are a feminist...?]*
> Their views.//...Not sitting round Greenham Common or anything like that (laughs).
>
> Ruth Richards, aged 17 (G3)

Only one woman of the oldest cohort expressed concern about the reception feminists get from the public and the media. Rene Evans (aged 82, G1) said that she regarded feminist women as 'very brave' because 'the bulk of the vote goes against them'.

The other important aspect of the vocabulary constructing feminism as commendable was the characterisations of feminists, an aspect especially found within the accounts of the oldest cohort. A particular feature was the attribution of admirable personality traits, such as assertiveness and authority and 'meaning what she says'. For example:

> *[Do you think Mrs Thatcher is a woman's libber?]*
> Yes, to a certain extent.// Well, her authority, for one.
>
> Nora Lestor, aged 72 (G1)

> *[Is there anyone who you would say was a feminist...?]*
> Margaret Thatcher.// Because she is really strong and she tries to sort things out in society and that...
>
> Mandy Mitchell, aged 17 (G3)

Other prominent women politicians (including Edwina Currie) were also identified as women's liberationists on the basis of their assertiveness and 'steadfastness'. Feminist women were thus seen as empowered role-models, who through their example, have broken new ground for women as a whole:

> Well, Margaret Thatcher has proved, hasn't she, I think she has proved it, being the first woman Prime Minister, she's proved it.
>
> Janet Morgan, aged 47 (G2)

For three women of the youngest cohort, however, Mrs. Thatcher was not representative of feminist women, because feminist women help other women and Mrs. Thatcher had not done so. Other sympathetic characterisations included identifying family members or friends as being feminists or women's liberationists, and here qualities such as being 'total individuals', and having an independent frame of mind featured.

One further aspect of the feminism as commendable vocabulary was the unreserved enthusiasm conveyed especially by some women of the middle cohort. Here, superlatives were used to portray the high regard in which they held feminism and feminists.

> I think it's a great thing. You know, more power to their elbow.
> Angharad Baker, aged 50 (G2)

> I think it's an excellent thing. Yes.
> Rosemary Thomas, aged 46 (G2)
> I think it's wonderful (laughs).
> Cynthia Daniels, aged 53 (G2)

Unlike the middle cohort, few women of the youngest cohort were so enthusiastic. They did not describe the women's movement as 'wonderful' or 'an excellent thing' but instead tended to describe it merely as 'good'. The most enthusiastic accounts of the youngest cohort were given by Hayley Baker and Isabel Ascote:

> *[What do you think of feminism?]*
> Well, I think it is a very important - if you can call it a point of view, I don't know. I think every woman should be a feminist.
> Hayley Baker, aged 23 (G3)

> *[Would you say that feminism is relevant to the way you think about the world or the things you try to do?]*
> The way I think. Yeah, definitely. Definitely. It has been a very, very large influence on my life...it has shaped my attitudes and ideas...it has been one of the largest single influences in my life. Definitely.
> Isabel Ascote, aged 21 (G3)

No women of the oldest cohort responded to feminism in a way that could be categorised as 'enthusiastic'. This, along with the findings that none introduced the topic of feminism (or women's liberation) themselves during the course of their interviews and only two identified themselves as feminists, further suggests that feminism was largely an irrelevant concept for the women of the oldest cohort.

In sum, sympathetic vocabularies constructed feminism as a moderate, progressive, beneficial and largely successful development, with commendable aims, objectives and outcomes. Women identified as feminists were described as individuals who were authoritative and compelling, who were empowered and who assisted other women. Of the three cohorts, the middle responded to feminism with considerable enthusiasm whilst the oldest were the most cool towards it.

Conclusions

Analyses undertaken in this chapter have indicated the importance of cohort in shaping responses to feminism and its influence on the language used to convey these responses, including the very terms 'feminism' and 'women's liberation'. Of the three cohorts, the oldest emerged as the least familiar with and least sympathetic toward feminism. It was the youngest cohort who conveyed the most familiarity with feminism and who, in many respects, emerged as the most sympathetic toward it.

All but one of the oldest cohort did not know what 'feminism' meant and three did not know what 'women's liberation' was either. Compared to younger cohorts, the oldest cohort seemed hesitant and vague in the attribution of aims and concerns to women's liberation. No women of this cohort independently introduced the issue of women's liberation during their interview and only two were prepared to identify themselves as women's liberationists in one way or another. In their accounts of women's liberation, whether hostile or sympathetic, responses were often 'individualised', in that the personality of women believed to be feminists was an especial focus. For those who used a vocabulary which constructed feminism as extremism, its adherents were described as having unpleasant personal qualities, such as 'dominance' or bossiness'. For those who used a vocabulary which constructed feminism as commendable, its adherents were similarly ascribed with 'strong' personalities but these were more positively labelled and regarded.

Familiarity with the term 'feminism' was much greater amongst the middle cohort, compared to the oldest cohort. However, seven of these women did not know what 'feminism' was and one also said that she did not know what 'women's liberation' was, either. The middle cohort appeared confident in the attribution of 'equality' as the principle concern of feminism. Seven women independently raised the issue of feminism during the course of their interviews and seven were also prepared to identify themselves as feminists in one way or another. Sympathy for the women's movement was conveyed through a vocabulary which portrayed feminism as commendable and several women of this cohort reported their admiration in an especially enthusiastic manner. Hostile vocabularies were also employed and especially that which constructed feminism as contrary to femininity.

All but three women of the youngest cohort knew what 'feminism' was and these women all knew what 'women's liberation' was. The youngest cohort attributed a wide range of concerns to feminism, including the sexual objectification of women. The greater familiarity of these women with feminism, compared to the older cohorts, was further evident in the finding that they drew distinctions between different types of feminism and feminists. Seven women independently raised the issue of feminism during the course of their interviews and eleven defined themselves as feminists in one way or another. In their accounts of feminism, hostile vocabularies were employed, and it was these women who especially constructed feminism (or at least, some versions of feminism) as being 'against men' and as contrary to femininity, via characterisation of feminists. Sympathy for the women's movement was conveyed through a vocabulary which portrayed feminism as commendable, although the language used to convey this response was less exuberant than found within some accounts of the middle cohort.

These differences in responses to feminism and variations in vocabularies used can be made sense of through locating the women's accounts in the context of their life courses and cohort membership. The oldest cohort of women had an average date of birth of 1915 and had, consequently, lived most of their lives when organised feminism was in abeyance, or characterised by a concern with 'welfare issues' (i.e. the 'new' feminism). These women were on average aged 55 when the 'second wave' of the women's movement emerged in the 1970s. Analyses undertaken in previous chapters have shown that, across a range of gender issues, the oldest cohort gave the most 'traditional' responses and were invariably 'hostile' to feminist constructions. The responses to gender issues by the oldest cohort and their lack of familiarity with the women's movement reflect the period in history through which they have lived. During their earlier lives, feminism was largely inaccessible, due to its low profile, whilst the 'second wave' of feminism must have seemed a development that was largely irrelevant to their own lives. Moreover, the findings reported in this chapter suggest that the oldest cohort of women have been excluded from full involvement in discussions about feminism in contemporary society, by the simple fact that they did not know what the term 'feminism' means.

The mainly sympathetic accounts of feminism given by the middle and youngest cohorts, and their greater familiarity with its vocabularies, aims and outcomes, also allow an interpretation in terms of socio-historical location. The two younger cohorts demonstrated the greatest familiarity with and enthusiasm for feminism. For the middle cohort, with an average date of birth of 1943, the period when the Women's Liberation Movement held a high public profile was likely to be part of their formative socialisation experiences. (Certainly, the references to 'bra burners' featured more in their accounts than in either of the other two cohorts). Their confident attribution of 'equality' as the main concern of feminism arguably reflected their exposure to the issue via the various pieces of 'equality legislation' introduced in the 1970s, as well as the marches and demonstrations which had equality as a focus. The youngest cohort, with an average date of birth of 1967, have lived most of their lives in a period characterised by the absence of a publicly visible, nationally organised women's' movement. Feminism in the 1980s and 1990s has been 'dispersed' and 'diffused' (Coote and Campbell 1987; Segal 1987) but influential. These women, in their education and employment, have arguably benefited from advances brought about by feminism. Consequently, these women showed the greatest degree of familiarity with feminism and its discourse.

Some differences in responses between the middle and youngest cohorts were apparent. First, it was the middle cohort who, when constructing feminism as commendable, were highly enthusiastic. Second, the youngest cohort were found to make distinctions between types of feminism and feminists. Arguably, these contrasting responses are also reflective of cohort membership. The youngest cohort were more reserved in expressing enthusiasm for feminism because they took feminism for granted, more so than women of the middle cohort. Moreover, their greater coolness may have reflected their greater awareness of the pejorative connotations of feminism, as indicated by the divisions they made between moderate, mainstream feminism and extreme 'hard', 'left-wing' or 'ultra' feminism. In other words, the lack of avid enthusiasm for feminism and the careful delineation of 'strengths' of feminism by the youngest cohort reflected the extent to which the basic tenets of feminism formed part of their world view, a world view which itself is a consequence of their socialisation experiences arising from their date of birth.

In their responses to interview questions on feminism, few women of each cohort gave wholly sympathetic or wholly hostile accounts; hence these were earlier described as 'mainly' hostile or sympathetic. In other words, on this issue, there was a notable tendency for the women to employ a mixture of hostile and sympathetic vocabularies. This indicates that feminism was responded to with a fair amount of ambivalence by the women, of all ages. Within vocabularies hostile to the women's movement, and those sympathetic toward it, there emerged less distinctive variations by cohort than was apparent on other issues. Yet, cohort clearly affected the women's responses to feminism, as indicated by for example, the proportion giving mainly hostile or mainly sympathetic accounts, the proportions defining themselves as a feminist and by the contrasting degrees of familiarity with the very term 'feminism' itself. In sum, within the accounts of feminism given by the three cohorts of women, it is possible to detect their contrasting socio-historical exposures to the organised women's movement and to feminism as a pervasive, influential ideology. Moreover, the finding that it was women of younger cohorts rather than those of older cohorts who responded more knowledgeably and sympathetically to feminism, is in keeping with the cohort patterns revealed in the preceding chapters. The degree of congruence of the findings are further considered in the concluding chapter, which, amongst other issues, also reflects upon the significance of age as a key social division, in the light of findings reported in this book.

Notes

1. The term originated in the belief that, as part of a protest against the 1968 Miss America contest, feminists discarded symbols of repressive femininity, including bras, and burned them. The burning never actually happened. However, references to 'bra burning' featured in six out of the nineteen accounts of the middle cohort of women, compared to only one example each in the accounts of the oldest and the youngest cohorts. Few of the women using 'bra burning' were able to talk about its significance or symbolic nature and thus it formed part of their understanding of the women's movement in the sense of being an image they held of it.

2. American evidence on responses to the women's movement is a little more plentiful. See, for example, Tavris (1973), Welch (1975), Andersen (1987), Renzetti (1987), Stacey (1987), Cowan *et al* (1992).

3. For a detailed discussion of the women's responses to Mrs. Thatcher, see Pilcher 1995a.

8. Conclusions

Cohort is an important predictor of attitudes on gender issues, as a number of surveys have shown. The qualitative study reported on in this book found that women responded to a range of gender issues in ways suggested by cohort studies with a quantitative design. In other words, women of the oldest cohort were found to give accounts of gender issues which were more traditional, less egalitarian, less liberal and less 'feminist' than women in the younger cohorts. As noted in the introductory chapter, the main concern of the study was, however, to extend understandings of cohort differences. It was hoped that the detailed examination of words and phrases would reveal cohort differences in the ways women *talk* about gender; in other words, differences in the 'vocabularies of motive' employed by women according to their cohort, which may be masked by quantitative studies. In many respects, the study attempted to put Mannheim's theory of social generations, discussed in Chapter One, in to practice, via a research strategy acknowledging its roots in the sociology of knowledge and the qualitative methodological implications of this. In this concluding chapter, I describe the overall patterns of the study's findings, arguing that they lead to the identification of a cohort-based 'unity of outlook', which acts to divide the women in terms of their constructions of gender issues and their responses to feminism. The implications of the study's findings, for cohort and social generation theory, for the qualitative investigation of the impact location in historical time has on social outlook and for knowledge about responses to gender issues and feminism, are also considered.

In the preceding chapters, analyses focused on the identification of sets of vocabularies given in response to open-ended interview questions on a range of gender issues. Following Mannheim, the study took the women's vocabularies as the empirical location or repository of their 'social generational consciousness' or world view. The ways in which the women talked about the various issues were used to 'locate' their world views within what was known about their likely formative socio-historical contexts. Following Mills, vocabularies were recognised to be subject to constraint, via cohort location in historical time and the 'dominant reference group' about whose opinion the actor cares. For each cohort, these constraints acted to make some ways of talking about gender issues both more available and more conventional (or acceptable) than others. The findings show that, on the gender issues raised in the interviews with the women, there co-existed a number of vocabularies, the use of which was often circumscribed by cohort membership. This acted either to restrict (or even prevent) access to a particular way of talking, or to make a particular vocabulary set inappropriate or unacceptable. The patterns of findings discussed in earlier chapters leads to the identification of two broad groupings of vocabularies used by the women, 'unities of outlook' which are reflective of the circumscribing circumstances arising from cohort location in historical time. *Traditionalist vocabularies* conveyed an orientation to past cultural practices on gender issues and a disdain of present cultural practices. Examples of traditionalist vocabularies include speaking of 'a woman's place' and of 'a man's place', of denying that women should be equal to men, and the description of homosexuality as a pathological affliction. *Progressive vocabularies* conveyed an orientation to present cultural practices on gender issues and a toleration and advocation of change, along with a disdain of past cultural practices. Examples of progressive vocabularies include approval of role reversal, the advocation of equality of opportunity in employment and a disdain of continuing inequalities, toleration of homosexuality on the grounds of individual rights and support for abortion via the notion that women have rights over their own bodies.

In comparison with the two younger cohorts of women, the oldest emerged as the most traditionalist and least egalitarian, liberal or feminist, in terms of the vocabularies they made use of. On each gender issue reported on in this book (except one), it was found that women of the oldest cohort tended to make use of vocabularies which can be described as 'traditionalist' in outlook. Thus, in their accounts of role reversal, the oldest cohort tended to make use of vocabularies of traditional gender roles and expressed a particular concern about the feelings and status of men. On the issue of equality and discrimination outside the domestic arena, they tended to report that equality had been achieved in contemporary society, in opposition to the feminist vocabulary of inequality. Some women also used a vocabulary of essential difference, which denied that men and women should or could be equal. On the issue of abortion, the oldest cohort were heavily disapproving, with several allowing no mitigating circumstances whatsoever and others restricting abortion to traumatic circumstances only. When talking about homosexuality, the tendency was to employ a pathological vocabulary, which portrayed homosexuality as 'against nature'. Several exhibited a reluctance to talk about the issue at all. The only issue on which these women tended to use vocabularies in sympathy with feminism was that of representations of women's bodies, via the example of Page Three. Here, they made use of moralist and feminist vocabularies to express their hostility toward Page Three. Whilst this finding may at first appear inconsistent, the vocabularies employed by the oldest cohort women when talking about Page Three were in keeping with their traditionalist world view, evident elsewhere. As argued in Chapter Six, their accounts of Page Three were congruent with what is known about their likely formative socio-historical experiences. The oldest cohort's tendency towards the use of vocabularies in opposition to those of feminism was found to be in keeping with their accounts of the women's movement. Specifically, they were found to lack familiarity with feminism (including this very term itself) and many expressed hostility toward the movement and its adherents. In sum, the oldest cohort's accounts of gender issues and the women's movement corresponded with what is known about their likely formative socio-historical experiences. Within this cohort of women, it is possible to identify a social generational consciousness or a unity of outlook which is traditionalist in character, and which is in accordance with what is known about its likely formative social contexts.

Within his theory of social generations, Mannheim makes the point that the process of social change is made smoother by the continuous transition from one social generation to another. He writes that '...it is not the oldest generation who meet the youngest at once; the first contacts are made by other "intermediary" generations, less removed from each other' (1952: 301). In this study of three cohorts of women and gender issues, it was found that, generally, the middle cohort did indeed have the characteristic of an intermediary or 'buffer' cohort, between the two 'pole' cohorts. On almost all of the gender issues reported in this book, and in their accounts of the women's movement *per se*, the middle cohort were found to make use of a mix of vocabularies which were in-between the greater traditionalism of the oldest and the greater progressiveness of the youngest cohorts. As data in Tables One to Six indicate, majorities in terms of whether the middle cohort's accounts were 'hostile' or 'sympathetic' were often very small. The frequently equivocal nature of the responses of the middle cohort can be interpreted in terms of their status as an intermediary cohort. On the whole, though, the middle cohort tended to demonstrate a greater similarity with the youngest cohort, in terms of the vocabularies they employed (such as individualist and feminist vocabularies). In other words, the division in this study was especially between the oldest cohort (aged 62-87) and the younger cohorts (aged 38-56 and 17-29), rather than a marked three-fold division, with the middle cohort in-between, as commonly reported in cohort surveys. In many ways, then, the middle cohort emerged as the most sociologically interesting, since their social generational consciousness was rather more fragmentary than either of the others. One way of making sense of disunified world views, particularly evident amongst the middle cohort, is via Mannheim's notion of 'social generation units' (see Chapter One). Mannheim recognised that within social generations, there may come in to being differing or opposing responses to the particular historical situation. Consequently, groups within a social generation may 'work up the material of their common experiences in different and specific ways' (1952: 304), so as to constitute separate social generation units. This may explain why some women of the middle cohort tended towards more traditionalist vocabularies (for example, Gwen Keating and Carol Mitchell) whilst others tended towards more progressive individualist and feminist vocabularies (Janice Caswell and Maureen Richards, for example).

The only issue on which a majority of middle cohort women did not give accounts comprised of vocabularies sympathetic to the feminist world view was that of Page Three. Here, a majority gave accounts sympathetic to Page Three whilst feminism is generally hostile to it. Although this finding may at first seem inconsistent, as explained in Chapter Six, it was in keeping with their tendencies toward progressive world views, evident on other issues. On some issues, the women of the middle cohort emerged as the most feminist-leaning of the three cohorts. As shown in Chapter Three, women of the middle cohort were the most likely to say that gender equality had yet to be achieved and that further improvements were needed. On the issue of abortion, it was women of the middle rather than the youngest cohort who employed an explicitly feminist vocabulary in their sympathetic accounts. Finally, as shown in the previous chapter, it was women of the middle cohort were who the most openly enthusiastic about feminism as an admirable force for change. These findings may point to the importance of the second wave of the women's movement in the 1960s and 1970s, which was part of the formative socialisation experiences of many of these women. For women of this cohort, an active campaigning movement was a direct experience during their teenage and early adult years and this is arguably reflected in their use of vocabularies on some issues and in aspects of their responses to feminism. Therefore, within this cohort of women, it is possible to identify a distinctive social generational consciousness, even if this is less unified in outlook than exhibited by the other cohorts. It is fully reflective of their location in historical time, in particular their exposure to a turbulent period of change in the gender order, including the renewal of feminist campaigning in the 1960s and 1970s.

The youngest cohort of women generally emerged as the least traditionalist and most progressive of the three groupings, as evidenced by the vocabularies they made use of. On the issue of role reversal, even in the minority of accounts hostile to it, reference was made to role reversal in terms of gender equality. Structural constraints restricting its likelihood were identified. Vocabularies of feminism and individualism were especially associated with these women, including on issues of abortion and homosexuality. Such vocabularies are in keeping with what is known about their likely formative socio-historical experiences. In all but two cases, a majority of the youngest cohort gave accounts which were sympathetic toward feminist world views. The first of these exceptions was the issue of gender equality, where those who said it had largely been achieved had a majority of one over those who said it had not. This rather equivocal position on the attainment of equality is arguably reflective both of their stage in life course, which may have restricted their experience of discrimination in employment and leisure, and their exposure to post-feminist rhetoric with its insistence that gender inequality has largely been eradicated. The second issue where the youngest cohort did not give accounts in accordance with the feminist position was that of Page Three. As noted above, Page Three also proved to be the 'odd one out' of the trend in the accounts of the oldest and middle cohorts. As I will argue shortly, this finding indicates that on the issue of representations of women as sexual objects, feminism has not been completely successful in getting its message across to younger women. Overall, the youngest cohort of women emerged as the most familiar with and the most sympathetic toward the women's movement, being (for example), the most likely to describe themselves as feminists. Taking the patterns of findings across the gender issues and the nature of the vocabularies employed in discussing them, the youngest cohort can therefore be recognised as having a social generational consciousness that is progressive in character and in keeping with what is known about their likely formative socialisation experiences.

There are a number of implications that can be drawn from the findings of this study. First, in relation to theory which emphasises the key role played by cohort and social generational processes in shaping socio-political orientations. The design of this study was directly informed by theory, specifically Mannheim's, which emphasises cohort as a fundamental influence on socio-political orientations. As noted in the introductory chapter, whilst cohort theory is 'extremely valuable in sensitising us to forces that we are prone to forget or ignore' (Rosow 1978: 74), empirical evidence for the various components of the theory is mixed. This is particularly true in relation to the distinctive feature of social generation as a concept: the idea that, once formed during the key period of youth, a person's cohort-based socio-political outlook is fixed and unchanging throughout their subsequent lives. The findings of the present study do support the idea that women construct gender issues in contrasting ways according to their cohort location in historical time, and that they retain distinctive world views as a result. The distinction between cohort (as a grouping sharing a calendar span of history in which they were born and grow through) and social generation (as a cohort grouping with distinctive and lasting ideological features, resulting from their shared socialisation experiences) is therefore a valid and sustainable one. In their accounts of gender issues, it is possible to identify the 'fresh contact' first the middle and then the youngest cohort has had with the pre-existing gender heritage, and their novel and distinctive approaches to gender divisions. The pattern of findings suggest that future cohorts of older women will experience their later life informed by progressive vocabularies of motive on gender matters, thereby accelerating and propelling further social change.

However, the findings of this study also suggest that cohort location and social generational consciousness are not immune from the influence of other contingencies. For example, in accounts of role reversal given by women of the oldest cohort, direct knowledge of role reversal successes seemed an important factor in shaping sympathetic accounts. On this issue at least, it would seem that knowledge of success can act to challenge and change some older women's ideas about gender. Similarly, survey data on attitudes to abortion discussed in Chapter Four indicates that on this issue, attitudes have become more liberal across all cohorts. Such findings indicate that social generational outlooks are not as fixed and inflexible as Mannheim's theory suggests. Family socialisation may also have affected cohort differences. Some families of women in the sample (for example, the Ascotes) were more 'progressive' than others (for example, the Keatings). Here, as suggested by Moen *et al* (1997), older generations may be 'socialised' by their daughters and grand-daughters and therefore shift away from their historically influenced world views towards a more progressive position. Furthermore, stage in life course may act to differentiate within cohorts. For example, although some had, many of the youngest cohort had not yet formed an independent household nor had they any children. These contingencies may have affected responses to the domestic division of labour (see also Pilcher 1994) and the construction of abortion and equality as gender issues. Finally, cohort and social generation seemed to have stronger effects on some issues rather than others. In accounts of Page Three for example, there appeared fewer quantitative and qualitative differences between the cohorts than was apparent on other issues. This arguably reflects the extent to which, on this issue, there exist strongly competing discourses (moral and feminist) which nonetheless share a degree of congruence with one another, acting to dissipate cohort effects. In sum, on the basis of this study, I concur with the conclusions reached by Alwin and his colleagues (1991). In other words, my findings support the broad emphasis of the 'cohort-persistence' model. However, it seems likely that the model, and cohort theory more generally, needs modification to allow for interaction between cohort processes and other variables, including those which may act, on some issues, to fragment any 'unity of outlook' based on cohort. At the least, more detailed consideration needs to be given to those aspects of Mannheim's theory which allow for the internal differentiation of social generations, through 'cultural location', 'social generation units' and the 'tempo of social change', for example.

A further set of implications relate to the potential for the qualitative investigation of location in historical time and social outlook. At the beginning of this book, it was noted that despite its roots in the sociology of knowledge, and an emphasis on the interpretation of meaning via a focus on language, most research on cohort (or more specifically, social generations) has been conducted via surveys. These are well-placed to explore the interrelation between cohort and other variables, can claim representativeness and generalisability of findings, and can identify degrees of cohort differences which are statistically significant. However, qualitative studies are better placed than quantitative studies when the concern is to explore differences in the ways agreement or disagreement may be expressed according to cohort. My argument is that findings from qualitative studies, such as reported on here, are an important supplement to surveys of cohort differences in women's gender attitudes. Qualitative studies are better placed to reveal the varied and complex ways women of different cohorts construct gender issues and the influence cohort has on the very language they use to do so. As shown in the analyses of accounts of role reversal, women in older and younger cohorts did not express their hostility or sympathy for the idea in the same ways. In hostile accounts, older women revealed a concern with men's status and feelings, whilst the needs of children for mothers was an important feature of hostile accounts given by the youngest cohort. As shown in Chapter Four, younger cohorts may be more favourable to abortion than older cohorts but cohort also acted to shape the language used to construct favourable accounts. In this study, it was found that middle cohort women directly constructed abortion as a gender issue via their use of a feminist vocabulary. Youngest cohort women were similarly supportive of abortion but tended to employ a gender-neutral vocabulary of individualism. In Chapter Five, it was shown that even where oldest cohort women were sympathetic toward homosexuals, this was expressed via a pathological vocabulary which was not found in the sympathetic accounts of the younger cohorts. A clear example of the way in which cohort influences language is provided by the marked contrast in familiarity with the term 'feminism' between the women, with only one oldest cohort woman knowing what it meant compared to sixteen youngest cohort women.

The study has also shown the important contribution a qualitative study can make to unravelling the complexities of responses to gender issues according to cohort. Whilst surveys can give proportions agreeing or disagreeing with a particular questionnaire item, it is often impossible to get a sense of the 'reasoning' in relation to gender that resulted in the reported agreement or disagreement. In Chapter Two, it was shown that more in the oldest cohort were hostile to role reversal compared to the younger cohorts. However, via the examination of the vocabularies through which this hostility was expressed, it became clear that gender was in many ways a more relevant category for the older cohort than it was for the younger cohorts. Via their use of a traditional vocabulary, the oldest cohort expressed a concern about the status and position of men under circumstances of role reversal. In contrast, via their use of a vocabulary of individualism, gender was largely an irrelevant consideration for women of the younger cohorts. In short, the study has shown that a qualitative approach is both possible and worthwhile: location in socio-historical time has been shown to effect the very ways in which vocabularies are employed by women in their accounts of gender issues.

Whilst this study has indicated the value of a qualitative approach in the examination of cohort and social generation, its findings also enhance sociological knowledge about women's constructions of gender issues and their responses to feminism. Having argued that, on the whole, the two younger cohorts in the study were more progressive in their accounts of gender issues than the oldest, and that feminist vocabularies featured in these progressive accounts, I do not mean to imply that feminism was therefore an unproblematically accessible or permissible world view for these women. Whilst this study has shown that feminism had entered in to the world views of younger cohorts of women, as evidenced by the way they talked about gender issues, it is also clear that feminism *per se* was viewed with some inconsistency and ambiguity. The comparison of findings on role reversal (Chapter Two) and equality (Chapter Three) showed that, across the cohorts, equality was regarded as a concept more appropriate to the 'public sphere' than the 'private sphere'. Whilst feminism has apparently succeeded in making formal, public, gender equality universally regarded as a 'good thing', it has clearly had less success inserting such discourses within domestic and personal relationships. Data discussed in the chapters reporting women's accounts of equality and of the organised women's movement also point to tensions between femininity and feminism for some women. In some women's accounts of equality, there emerged a concern with 'being treated like a woman', a preference which was held to contradict with feminist convictions. Similarly, in accounts of the characteristics of feminist women, an apparent lack of femininity emerged as a strong theme, via a vocabulary which posited feminism as contrary to femininity.

All issues raised with the women in the interviews were recognisably gender issues, and ones which feminism has identified as problematical. Yet, explicitly feminist vocabularies were rarely employed, in comparison with the prominence of the more neutral individualist vocabularies. On many of the gender issues reported in this book, including those of abortion and role reversal, individualism often appeared to be a more accessible and permissible vocabulary with which to construct progressive accounts. Moreover, where explicitly feminist vocabularies were employed, this was often in the accounts of the middle, as opposed to the youngest, cohort. As argued in Chapter Seven, this may have been a reflection of the younger cohort's greater sensitivity to the pejorative connotations of feminism. For the two younger cohorts of women in this study, the language and ideology of individualism seemed to have a greater influence than for the older, a trend noted to be taking place at the macro level as the century progresses (Lukes 1973; Hutson and Jenkins 1989). It would appear, on the basis of this study, that individualism is a more accessible and appropriate vocabulary of motive than feminism, even when the issues under discussion are explicitly feminist ones. In particular, the findings on accounts of Page Three strongly suggest that where feminist principles conflict with issues of personal choice and freedom, feminism loses support amongst younger women. Whilst both ideologies can be viewed as progressive, the prevalence of individualism over feminism means that the collective oppression of women on the basis of their gender loses prominence, along with recognition of structures of patriarchy and practices of sexism. The findings of this study point to future cohorts of women being even more progressive than the youngest cohort in this study (that is, if the pattern found of older cohorts being less progressive than younger ones is repeated; evidence indicates that this is the direction of change). However, the findings also show that future cohorts of women might not express their progressive world views, even on matters directly concerned with gender, with a vocabulary of feminism.

Whilst this study has demonstrated the influence of social generation in terms of accounts women gave about gender issues and feminism, there remains much work to be done within the wider area of the sociology of age and the sociology of knowledge in terms of social generations. The research reported here was restricted in its scope in that it was undertaken in Wales (a region shown in surveys to be more traditionalist in outlook than other areas of Britain; see Jowell *et al* 1988, table 8.6), with a small sample of women, with principal attention paid to the role of social generation rather than class, employment status or education. Other studies might consider the interaction of these variables with social generation. An obvious subsequent study would be a parallel study of the accounts three generations of men give about gender issues: are the future partners of contemporary young women also more progressive, egalitarian and feminist than their fathers and grandfathers?

As a discipline, sociology has rightly been concerned with the analysis of economic and power structures, including class, 'race' and gender, and how these act upon the everyday lives of individuals. The findings of this book point to the importance of recognising that societies are also stratified by time (Adam 1990), in the sense of cohort location in socio-historical structures. Age therefore needs fully to be recognised to be as a fundamental source of diversity and difference among women, alongside class and ethnicity (see also Pilcher 1995b). To paraphrase Troll (1970), contemporaneous women may share the same gender, and be living at the same time, but they do not share the same history and this leads them to interpret, define and give meaning to social reality in varied and contrasting ways.

Bibliography

Abbott, P. and Sapsford, R. (1987) *Women and Social Class*, Tavistock, London.

Abercrombie, N. (1980) *Class, Structure and Knowledge. Problems in the Sociology of Knowledge*, Basil Blackwell, Oxford.

Abrams, P. (1972) 'Age and Generation' in Barker, P. (ed.) *A Sociological Portrait*, Penguin, Harmondsworth.

Adam, B. (1990) *Time and Social Theory*, Polity/Basil Blackwell, Oxford.

Airey, C. and Brook, L. (1986) 'Interim Report: Social and Moral Issues' in Jowell, R. , Witherspoon, L. and Brook, L. (eds) *British Social Attitudes. The 1986 Report*, Gower, Aldershot.

Alberti, J. (1989) *Beyond Suffrage. Feminists in War and Peace 1914-1928*, MacMillan, London.

Alwin, D. and Scott, J. (1996) 'Attitude Change: its measurement and interpretation using longitudinal surveys' in Taylor, B. and Thomson, K. (eds) *Understanding Change in Social Attitudes*, Dartmouth, Aldershot.

Alwin, D., Cohen, R., and Newcomb, T. (1991) *Political Attitudes Over the Life Span. The Bennington Women After Fifty Years*, University of Wisconsin Press, Wisconsin.

Andersen, M.L. (1987) 'Corporate Wives: Longing for Liberation or Satisfied with the Status Quo?' in Deegan, M.J. and Hill, M. (eds), *Women and Symbolic Interaction*, Allen Unwin, London.

Assister, A. and Carol, A. (1993, eds.) *Bad Girls and Dirty Pictures*, London, Pluto.

Banks, Olive (1981) *Faces of Feminism. A study of feminism as a social movement*, Martin Robertson, Oxford.

Beddoe, D. (1989) *Back to Home and Duty. Women Between the Wars 1918-1939*, Pandora, London.

Bell, M and Schwede, K (1985) 'Roles, Feminist Attitudes and Older Women', *Women and Politics*, vol 5, 1, 5-22.

Bengston, V.L., Furlong, M.J., and Laufer, R.S. (1974) 'Time, Aging and the Continuity of Social Structure: Themes and Issues in Generational Analyisis', *Journal of Social Issues*, vol. 39, 4, 45-72.

Blumer, H. (1969) *Symbolic Interactionism. Perspective and Method*, Prentice-Hall, New Jersey.

Bott, E. (1971) *Family and Social Network. Roles, Norms and External Relationships in Ordinary Urban Families*, London: Tavistock (first published 1957).

Brannen, J. and Moss, P. (1991) *Managing Mothers. Dual Earner Households after Maternity Leave*, Unwin Hyman, London.

Braungart, M.M. (1984) 'Aging and Politics', *Journal of Military and Political Sociology*, vol. 12, pp 79-98.

Braybon, G. and Summerfield, P. (1987) *Out of the Cage. Women's Experiences in Two World Wars*, Pandora, London.

Brennan, T., Cooney, E.W., and Pollins, H. (1954) *Social Change In South West Wales*, Watts and Co., London.

Buss, A. (1974) 'Generational Analysis: Description, Explanation and Theory', *Journal of Social Issues*, vol. 30, 2, 55-72.

Campaign for Family and Womanhood (1988-9) *Vive La Difference*, 16, Winter.

Central Statistical Office (1995) *Social Focus on Women*, The Stationery Office, London.

Charvet, J. (1982) *Feminism*, J.M. Dent and Sons, London.

Collinson, D., Knights, D. and Collinson, M. (1990) *Managing to Discriminate*, Routledge, London.

Coote, A. and Campbell, B. (1987) *Sweet Freedom. The Struggle for Women's Liberation*, 2nd edition, Basil Blackwell, Oxford.

Cowan, G., Mestlin, M. and Masek, J. (1992) 'Predictors of Feminist Self-Labelling', *Sex Roles*, vol. 27, pp 321-330.

Cowan, R. Schwartz (1989) *More Work for Mother. The Ironies of Household Technology from the Open Hearth to the Microwave*, Free Association Books, London.

Coward, R. (1987) 'Sexual Violence and Sexuality' in Feminist Review (ed), *Sexuality: A Reader*, Virago, London.

Crane, P. (1982) *Gays and the Law*, Pluto Press, London.

Crook, R. (1982) 'Tidy Women. Women In the Rhondda Between the Wars', *Oral History*, vol.10, 2, 40-57.

Dant, T. (1991) *Knowledge, Ideology and Discourse. A Sociological Perspective*, Routledge, London.

Delamont, S. (1980) *The Sociology of Women*, George Allen and Unwin, London.

Delmar, R. (1986) 'What Is Feminism?' in Mitchell, J., and Oakley, A. (eds) *What is Feminism?*, Basil Blackwell, Oxford.

Dennis, N., Henriques, F., and Slaughter, C. (1969) *Coal is Our Life. An Analysis of a Yorkshire Mining Community*, 2nd edition, Tavistock, London (first published 1956).

Dyhouse, C. (1989) *Feminism and the Family in England 1880-1939*, Basil Blackwell. Oxford.

Emmison, M. and Western, M. (1990) 'Social Class and Social Identity: A Comment on Marshall *et al*', *Sociology* vol. 24, 2, 241-253.

Esler, A. (1984) ' "The Truest Community": Social Generations as Collective Mentalities', *Journal of Political and Military Sociology*, vol.12, 99-112.

Faludi, S. (1992) *Backlash*, Chatto Windus, London.

Ferriman, A. (1991) 'Clinics Plan Over 4000 Abortions by Pill Method', *The Guardian*, 8th December.

Ferris, P. (1967) *The Nameless*, Penguin, Harmondsworth.

Finch, J. (1986) 'Age' in Burgess, R. (ed.) *Key Variables in Social Investigation*, RKP., London.

Frazer, E. (1988) 'Teenage Girls Talking About Class', *Sociology* vol. 22, 3, 343-358.

Gavron, H. (1983) *The Captive Wife. Conflicts of Housebound Mothers*, RKP., London (first published 1966).

Gershuny, J. (1997) 'The Changing Nature of Work'. Paper presented at the British Association Conference, Leeds, 8th September.

Glass, J., Bengtson, V., Chorn Dunham, C. (1986) 'Attitude Similarity in Three Generation Families: Socialisation, Status Inheritance or Reciprocal Influence', *American Sociological Review*, vol. 51, pp 685-698.

Greenwood, V. and Young, J. (1976) *Abortion in Demand*, Pluto, London.

Griffin, C. (1989), ' "I'm not a feminist but...": feminism, consciousness and identity', in Skevington. S. and Barker. D. (eds) *The Social Identitiy of Women*, Sage, London.

Hakim, C. (1987) *Research Design*, Allen and Unwin, London.

Hammersley, M. (1989) *The Dilemma of Qualitative Method. Herbert Blumer and the Chicago School*, Routledge, London.

Harding, S. (1988) 'Trends in Permissiveness' in Jowell, R., Witherspoon, S. and Brook, L. (eds) *British Social Attitudes*, Gower, Aldershot.

Heath, A. and Martin, J. (1996) 'Changing Attitudes Towards Abortion: Life-cycle, period and cohort effects' in Taylor, B. and Thomson, K. (eds) *Understanding Change in Social Attitudes*, Dartmouth, Aldershot.

Holdsworth, A. (1988) *Out of the Dolls House. The Story of Women in the Twentieth Century*, B.B.C., London.
Hunt, A. (1988) 'Women and Paid Work: Issues of Equality. An Overview' in Hunt, A. (ed.) *Women and Paid Work*, MacMillan, London.
Hutson, S. and Jenkins, R. (1989) *Taking the Strain. Families, Unemployment and the Transition to Adulthood*, Open University Press, Milton Keynes.
Itzin, C. (1992) 'Legislating Against Pornography Without Censorship' in Itzin, C. (ed.) *Pornography*, Oxford University Press, Oxford.
Jackson, E. (1995) 'The Problem with Pornography: a critical survey of the current debate', *Feminist Legal Studies*, vol. 3 (1), pp 49-70.
Jackson, S. and Scott, S. (1996) 'Sexual Skirmishes and Feminist Factions' in Jackson, S. and Scott, S. (eds) *Feminism and Sexuality. A Reader*, Edinburgh University Press, Edinburgh.
Johnson, A. (1988) 'Short's Page Three Bill secures a first reading', *The Guardian*, 14th April.
Jowell, R, Witherspoon, S. and Brook, L. (1988), (eds) *British Social Attitudes. The Fifth Report*, Gower, Aldershot.
Kalish, R.A. and Johnson, A.I. (1972) 'Value Similiarities and Differences in Three Generations of Women', *Journal of Marriage and the Family* vol. 34: 49-54.
Kent, S.K. (1988) 'The Politics of Sexual Difference: World War One and the Demise of British Feminism', *Journal of British Studies*, vol. 27: 232-253.
Kitzinger, C. (1987) *The Social Construction of Lesbianism*, Sage, London.
Knewstub, N. and Linton, M. (1990) 'Abortion Limit Cut to 24 Weeks', *The Guardian*, 25th April.
Landesman, C. (1997) 'Boy Zone', *The Guardian*, December 1st.
Laufer, R.S. and Bengston, V.L. (1974) 'Generations, Aging and Social Stratification: On the Development of Generational Units', *Journal of Social Issues*, vol. 30: 181-205.
Leonard, A. (1987) *Pyrrhic Victories: Winning Sex Discrimination and Equal Pay Cases in the Industrial Tribunal 1980-84*, Equal Opportunities Research Series, HMSO, London.
Lofland, J. and Lofland, L.H. (1984) *Analyzing Social Settings. A Guide to Qualitative Observation and Analysis*, Wadsworth, California.
Luker, K. (1984) *Abortion and the Politics of Motherhood*, University of California Press, Berkely.
Lukes, S. (1973) *Individualism*, Basil Blackwell, Oxford.
Lummis, T. (1982) 'The Historical Dimension of Fatherhood: A Case Study 1890-1914' in McKee, L. and O'Brien, M. (eds) *The Father Figure*, Tavistock, London.

Mannheim, K. (1952) 'The Problem of Generations' in Mannheim, K. *Essays on the Sociology of Knowledge*, R.K.P, London (first published 1923).

Mannheim, K. (1960) *Ideology and Utopia*, Routledge, London (first published 1936).

Mansfield, P., and Collard, J. (1988) *The Beginning of the Rest of Your Life? A Portrait of Newly-wed Marriage*, MacMillan, London.

Martin, J. and Roberts, C. (1984) *Women and Employment. A Lifetime Perspective*, H.M.S.O., London.

Mason, J. (1987) 'A Bed of Roses? Women, Marriage and Inequality in Later Life' in Allat, P., Keil, T., Bryman, A. and Bytheway, B. (eds) *Women and the Life Cycle*, MacMillan, London.

Mills, C. Wright (1967a) 'Situated Actions and Vocabularies of Motives' in Horowitz, I. (ed.) *Power, Politics and People. The Collected Essays of C. Wright Mills*, O.U.P., Oxford (first published 1940).

Mills, C. Wright (1967b) 'Language, Logic and Culture' in Horowitz, I. (ed.) *Power, Politics and People. The Collected Essays of C. Wright Mills*, O.U.P., Oxford (first published 1939).

Mills, C. Wright (1970) *The Sociological Imagination*, Penguin, London.

Misra, R. and Panigrahi, B. (1995) 'Change in Attitudes Towards Working Women: A Cohort Analysis', *International Journal of Sociology and Social Policy*, vol. 15: 1-20.

Moen, P., Erickson, M. and Dempster-McClain, D. (1997) 'Their Mother's Daughters? The Intergenerational Transmission of Gender Attitudes in a Changing World', *Journal of Marriage and the Family*, vol. 59: 281-293.

Mogey, J.M. (1956) *Family and Neighbourhood: Two Studies in Oxford*, O.U.P., Oxford.

Morgan. A. and Wilcox. C. (1992) 'Anti-feminism in Western Europe 1975-1987', *West European Politics,* vol. 15: 151: 169.

Morris, L. (1985a) 'Local Social Networks and Domestic Organisation: A Study of Redundant Steelworkers and their Wives', *Sociological Review*, vol. 33: 327-342.

Morris, L. (1985b) 'The Renegotiation of the Domestic Division of Labour in the Context of Male Redundancy' in Roberts, B., Finnegan, R. and Gallie, D. (eds) *New Approaches to Economic Life: Economic Restructuring, Unemployment and the Social Division of Labour*, M.U.P., Manchester.

Morris, L. (1985c) 'Renegotiation of the Domestic Division of Labour in the context of Male Redundancy' in Newby, H., Bujra, J., Littlewood, P., Rees, G., and Rees. T.L. (eds) *Restructuring Capital. Recession and Reorganization in Industrial Society*, Macmillan, London.

Morris, L. (1987) 'Constraints on Gender' *Work, Employment and Society*, vol. 1: 87-106.
Morris, L. (1990) *The Workings of the Household*, Polity, Cambridge.
Murcott, A. (1987) *Conceptions of Food. A Sociological Analysis*, unpublished Ph.D., University of Wales.
Nash, L. (1978) 'Greek Origins of Generational Thought', *Daedalus* 107, 1-22.
Neustatter, A. (1990) *Hyenas in Petticoats. A Look at Twenty Years of Feminism*, Penguin, Harmondsworth.
Oakley, A. (1974) *The Sociology of Housework*, Martin Robertson, London.
Office of National Statistics (1997) *Abortion Statistics 1995*, The Stationery Office, London.
Office of Population Census and Surveys (1980) *Classification of Occupations*, H.M.S.O., London.
Office of Population Census and Surveys (1985) *Abortion Statistics*, H.M.S.O, London.
Pahl, R. (1984) *Divisions of Labour*, Basil Blackwell, Oxford.
Petcheskey, R. (1986) *Abortion and Woman's Choice: The State, Sexuality and Reproductive Freedom*, Verso, London.
Pilcher, J. (1994) 'Who should do the dishes? Three Generations of Welsh Women Talking about Men and Housework' in Aaron, J., Rees, T., Betts, S., and Vincentelli, M. (eds) *Our Sisters' Land. The Changing Identities of Women in Wales,* University of Wales Press, Cardiff.
Pilcher, J. (1995a) 'The Gender Significance of Women in Power. British Women Talking About Margaret Thatcher', *European Journal of Women's Studies*, vol 2: 493-508.
Pilcher, J. (1995b) *Age and Generation in Modern Britain*, Oxford University Press, Oxford.
Plummer, K. (1983) *Documents of Life. An Introduction to the Problems and Literature of a Humanistic Method*, George Allen and Unwin, London.
Pursehouse, M. (1991) 'Looking at the Sun: into the nineties with a tabloid and its readers', *Cultural Studies from Birmingham,* vol.1.
Randall, V. (1982) *Women and Politics*, MacMillan, London.
Red Flannel Films (1988) *Mam*.
Renzetti, C. M. (1987) 'New Wave or Second Stage? Attitudes of College Women Toward Feminism' *Sex Roles*, vol. 16: 265-277.
Rice, D. (1971) 'The Roman Catholic View' in Medawar, J. and Pyke, D. (eds) *Family Planning*, Penguin, Harmondsworth.
Richardson, D. (1993) 'Sexuality and Male Dominance' in Richardson, D. and Robinson, V. (eds) *Introducing Women's Studies*, Macmillan, London.

Roberts, C. and Lang, K. (1985) 'Generations and Ideological Change: some observations', *Public Opinion Quarterly,* vol. 49: 460-473

Roberts, E. (1984) *A Woman's Place. An Oral History of Working Class Women, 1890-1940*, Basil Blackwell, Oxford.

Rodgerson, G. and Wilson, E. (1991), (eds) *Pornography and Feminism*, London, Lawrence and Wishart.

Roper, B.S. and Labeff, E. (1977) 'Sex Roles and Feminism Revisited. An Intergenerational Attitude Comparison', *Journal of Marriage and the Family*, vol. 39:113-119.

Rose, D. (1990) 'Crime puts women in state of seige' *The Guardian*, 13th March 1990.

Rosow, I. (1978) 'What is a Cohort and Why?', *Human Development*, vol. 21: 65-75.

Rosser C., and Harris, C. (1965) *The Family and Social Change. A Study of Family and Kinship in a South Wales Town*, R.K.P., London.

Rowland, R. (1984) *Women Who Do and Women Who Don't Join the Women's Movement*, R.K.P., London.

Schneider, B.E. (1988) 'Political Generations and the Contemporary Women's Movement', *Sociological Inquiry*, vol. 58: 4-21.

Schuman, H. and Rieger, C. (1992) 'Historical Analogies, Generational Effects and Attitudes Toward War', *American Sociological Review*, vol. 57: 315-326.

Schuman, H. and Scott, J. (1989) 'Generations and Collective Memories', *American Sociological Review*, vol. 54: 359-381.

Schwarz, W. and Sharatt, T. (1990) 'Stable Relationships...', *The Guardian*, 10 February.

Scott, J., Alwin, D. and Brown, M. (1996) 'Generational Changes in Gender Role Attitudes', *Sociology*, vol. 30: 471-492.

Sears, D. (1983) 'The Persistence of Early Political Predispositions. The roles of attitude and object and life stage' in Wheeler, L. and Shaver, P. (eds) *Review of Personality and Social Psychology*, vol. 4, Sage: Beverly Hills.

Segal, L. (1987) *Is the Future Female? Troubled Thoughts on Contemporary Feminism*, Virago, London.

Slevin, K.F. and Wingrove, C. Ray (1983) 'Similarities and Differences Among Three Generations of Women in Attitudes Toward the Female Role in Contemporary Society', *Sex Roles*, vol. 9: 609-624.

Smart, C. (1989) *Feminism and the Power of the Law*, Routledge, London.

Snell, M. (1986) 'Equal Pay and Sex Discrimination' in Feminist Review (eds) *Waged Work. A Reader*, Virago, London.

Spender, D. (1982) *There Has Always Been a Women's Movement This Century*, Pandora, London.

Spitzer, A.B. (1973) 'The Historical Problem of Generations', *American Historical Review* vol. 78: 1353-1385.

Stacey, J. (1987) 'Sexism By A Subtler Name? Post Industrial Conditions and Post Feminist Consciousness in the Silicon Valley', *Socialist Review* vol. 17: 7-28.

Stewart, A. and Healy, J.M. (1989) 'Linking Individual Development and Social Changes', *American Psychologist*, vol. 44: 30-42.

Tavris, C. (1973) 'Who Likes Women's Liberation - and Why: The Case of the Unliberated Liberals', *Journal of Social Issues*, vol. 29: 175-198.

Thomas, P. and Costigan, R. (1991) *Promoting Homosexuality: Section 28 of the Local Government Act 1988*, Cardiff Law School, Cardiff.

Thompson, P. (1975) *The Edwardians. The Remaking of British Society*, Weidenfeld and Nicolson, London.

Thornton, A., Alwin, D. and Camburn, D. (1983) 'Causes and Consequences of Sex Role Attitudes and Attitude Change', *American Sociological Review* vol. 48: 211-227.

Troll, L. (1970) 'Issues in the Study of Generations', *Aging and Human Development*, vol. 1: 78-89.

Tunks, K. and Hutchinson, D. (1991) *Dear Clare...This Is What Women Feel About Page 3*, Hutchinson Radius, London.

Tuttle, L (1986) *Encyclopedia of Feminism*, Harlow, Essex: Longman.

Walby, S. (1990) *Theorizing Patriarchy*, Basil Blackwell, Oxford.

Walby, S. (1993) ' "Backlash" in Historical Context' in Kennedy, M., Lubelska, C. and Walsh, V. (eds), *Making Connections*, Taylor and Francis, London.

Walby, S. (1997) *Gender Transformations*, Routledge, London.

Wandor, M. (1972), (ed.) *The Body Politic*, Stage One, London.

Wandor, M. (1990) *Once A Feminist. Stories of a Generation*, Virago, London.

Warde, A. and Hetherington K. (1993) 'A Changing Domestic Division of Labour? Issues of Measurement and Interpretation', *Work, Employment and Society* vol. 7: 23-45.

Warner, N. (1983) 'Parliament and the Law' in Galloway, B. (ed.) *Prejudice and Pride. Discrimination Against Gay People in Modern Britain*, R.K.P., London.

Weeks, J. (1985) *Sexuality and Its Discontents. Meanings, Myths and Modern Sexualities*, R.K.P., London.

Weeks, J. (1989) *Sex, Politics and Society*, Longman, London.

Welch, S. (1975) 'Support among women for the issues of the women's movement', *Sociological Quarterly*, vol. 16: 216-227.

Wellings, K., Field, J., Johnson, A. and Wadsworth, J. (1994) *Sexual Behaviour in Britain*, Penguin, London.

Wier, A. and Wilson, E. (1984) 'The British Women's Movement', *New Left Review*, vol. 148: 74-103.

Winckler, V. (1987a) 'Women and Work in Contemporary Wales', *Contemporary Wales*, vol. 1: 53-71.

Winckler, V. (1987b) 'Women in Post War Wales', *Llafur*, vol. 4: 69-77.

Witherspoon, S. (1985) 'Sex Roles and Gender Issues' in Jowell, R., and Witherspoon, S. (eds) *British Social Attitudes. The Fifth Report*, Gower, Aldershot.

Witherspoon, S. (1988) 'Interim Report: A Woman's Work' in Jowell, R., Witherspoon, S. and Brook, L. (eds.) *British Social Attitudes*, Gower, Aldershot.

Young, M. and Willmott, P. (1975) *The Symmetrical Family*,

Zweig, F. (1952) *Women's Life and Labour*, Victor Gollancz, London.